PERFORMANCE PLANNING & APPRAISAL

Patricia King

PERFORMANCE PLANNING & APPRAISAL

A How-To Book

for Managers

McGraw-Hill Book Company
New York   St. Louis   San Francisco   Auckland   Bogotá   Hamburg
London   Madrid   Mexico   Montreal   New Delhi
Panama   Paris   São Paulo   Singapore   Sydney   Tokyo   Toronto

Library Congress Cataloging in Publication Data

King, Patricia, date
   Performance Planning & Appraisal
   1. Employees, Rating of. I. Title.
HF5549.5.R3K53   1984   658.3'125   83-9831
ISBN 0-07-034631-3
ISBN 0-07-034640-2 (PBK.)

3 4 5 6 7 DOC/DOC 9 9 8 7 6 5 4 3 2 1 0

ISBN 0-07-034640-2 (PBK.)

The editors for this book were Rita Margolies and Philip McCaffrey, the designer was Jules Perlmutter, and the production supervisor was Reiko F. Okamura. It was set in Caledonia by Datagraphics.

Printed and bound by R. R. Donnelley & Sons Company.

For more information about other McGraw-Hill materials,
call 1-800-2-MCGRAW in the United States. In other
countries, call your nearest McGraw-Hill office.

In memory of
Annamarie Pisacane Puglise, my mother
Sister Mary Catharine O'Connor, my teacher

Contents

Preface

I spend my time teaching. In the conference rooms of corporations, managers and their subordinates tell me about the problems they have getting the work done.

What managers and employees seem to need is a way of accomplishing the work that allows them to be humane and still effective, a way that can lead to both high productivity and high job satisfaction. I am convinced that the techniques described in this book can produce these good results. The book does not describe a managerial style, but a procedure. You won't find advice here to be soft or to get tough. You will find a way to be fair.

If there is a philosophy behind this book, it is that performance planning and appraisal work best if the process preserves and enhances the individual dignity of both the manager and the employee and that managerial systems work best if they allow people to act according to enlightened self-interest. What this book describes is a system for controlling the work, not the people.

This is a book about performance appraisal, but it does not contain even one sample form. Despite its prevailing treatment in most organizations, performance appraisal is not about forms. It is about manager and employee coming to a clear understanding of what needs to be done, communicating frequently about progress, and finally appraising the results of their efforts. In other words, we are not talking about a once-a-year event. We are talking about an ongoing process, a way of managing for results.

It takes a lot to be a good manager. Libraries full of books have been written on the subject. Almost all of them contain good advice. This one does too. But to be a good manager, ultimately you need to want to be one. You need to want your people to think of you as a good manager. You need enthusiasm for the act of managing—not just for its rewards. And you must be willing to spend your time with the people who report to you, not just with the powerful people who are above you in the organization.

Planning, tracking, and evaluating the work of your people is an important part of what you must do as a manager. If you want to do these things really well, you will find a way. This book is intended as a practical manual to help you find that way. I hope it helps you. I think it will.

Pat King

Acknowledgments

Thank you to David Clark, my husband, and Kerry Ann King, my daughter; to Bill Newton, my first editor; to Bonnie Binkert, the McGraw-Hill editor who graciously adopted an orphan book; to Ann Darby, my friend and assistant; to Howard Denmark, Eileen and Tom Curtin, and Dick Hopple, who read the manuscript and were generous with their suggestions; to Bob Jud, John Davis, Paul McQuarry, Deborah Ness, and M. E. Nichols, who contributed their ideas. And to Vic S., who gave me my first performance appraisal and did it so badly, he convinced me that there must be a better way.

PERFORMANCE PLANNING & APPRAISAL

Chapter **1**

Introduction

Why Does Everyone Hate Performance Appraisal?

For many middle managers, the most popular decision their top managements could make about performance appraisal would be to abolish it. If you are one of those managers, I sympathize with you. Doing performance appraisal well is demanding, and many organizations have systems that further complicate the process. About three-fourths of U.S. corporations have formal performance appraisal systems, and more are instituting such systems every day. Yet few required activities elicit the negative response one hears when performance appraisal is mentioned. But don't despair. Your decision to read this book is the first step to understanding and getting comfortable (yes, I really mean comfortable) with performance appraisal. This book will give you an overview of performance appraisal so you can understand how it works and why it sometimes fails; even more important, you will get some practical advice for making your performance appraisals productive for you and your employees. The key words here are "productive" and "comfortable."

I feel very positive about the approach to performance appraisal described in this book, and I intend to treat the subject very positively. But it seems to me that we'd better deal with the objections first. When I told my friend Tom that I would be writing on this subject, he groaned. "If there's one thing," he said, "that makes me glad to be out of management and in my current staff job, it's performance appraisal. I hated that more than any other aspect of my job when I was a manager." Tom is a bright, conscientious, and energetic guy. What could cause him to be so negative? His feelings, I think, are fairly typical.

"One problem," Tom told me, "was the time it took. In my last management assignment, I had to do twenty-six performance appraisals in one year. Do you know how much time that required?" I haven't talked to many managers who are that overburdened with appraisals, but managers frequently complain about the time involved. And in a certain sense they are right. Doing a good job of performance appraisal takes time and energy. Some managers feel they have been investing too much. They usually feel that way because the payoff has not been worth the investment. When performance appraisal is done productively, its rewards can easily justify the investment. If the system you work with is cumbersome or if your own skills of planning, analysis, or communication are lacking, you should find this book helpful in getting more out of performance appraisal. But unless you are willing to give more than a token investment of energy in the process, the system is bound to fail.

Another difficulty with performance appraisal is the embarrassment managers feel when they have to evaluate an employee face to face. It makes people uncomfortable to sit in judgment of others. Managers worry about the response they will get: Will the person get angry and shout? Will there be a scene? Will the person start to cry? Won't this just ruin whatever rapport I've managed to build up since the last performance appraisal fiasco? Managers imagine the outcome of the appraisal meeting, and considering what they expect (or perhaps what they have experienced in the past), it's no wonder that they find the prospect unattractive. Unattractive? For some of us it's downright scary to think that something that is supposed to accomplish so much good could do so much harm.

And if managers feel a great burden of responsibility, they have good reason. Surveys of U.S. corporations indicate that in more than 90 percent of the companies, the employee's immediate supervisor is solely responsible for doing performance appraisal. Many managers have been asked to take this responsibility without much preparation. Often performance appraisal systems are announced and go into effect immediately. New forms are delivered; memos arrive detailing how the system will work and what the manager is expected to do. Perhaps there is a general meeting in the department to discuss the subject, but most organizations have not done a thorough job of training managers. For many of us, this lack of training has led to trial and error learning. For some, there have been enough errors and sour experiences to turn us off to the whole idea.

Another problem with performance appraisal is that the process often differs a great deal from what managers are comfortable with. Research shows that most managerial time is fragmented. Managers spend their days involved in brief, discrete episodes that have a distinct beginning and end. Managers become comfortable with this style of interacting. But when it is done well, performance appraisal is exactly the opposite. It is a continuous process that has considerable carry-over from one "encounter" to another. And for some managers, the boss-subordinate interaction, especially the frank conversation about problems, may "go against the grain." Managers whose personal style does not include this kind of communication feel uncomfortable with those aspects of performance appraisal that require it.

For a company or a department, the cooperation between manager and employee required by performance appraisal may be a departure from business as usual. Managers sense the inconsistency between the way the performance appraisal system requires them to behave and the way they customarily treat subordinates in the organization. Employees recognize the sharp contrasts too. Their involvement in goal setting and appraisal may be their only experience of participative management. Some employees respond very positively. But, if the employee is made suspicious by an apparent inconsistency and the manager is already uncomfortable, the results can be bad. The manager may wind up feeling manipulated by the system while the employee feels manipulated by the manager.

For some of us then, performance appraisal makes a lot of sense in theory but doesn't work in practice. Then again, some managers have not really put much effort into doing performance appraisals well. For instance, it is fairly common for supervisors and managers first to figure out what kind of raise or promotion they want to give someone and then to fill out the performance appraisal forms with the ratings that will get the raise approved.

Many managers view performance appraisal as a personnel department program. They feel that it's something they must do, but that it doesn't have a real payoff for them. Researchers in the field have found that only about one-fourth of the managers who have conducted performance appraisal meetings spent more than an hour in their discussions. It doesn't seem fair that a lot of managers short-change the process and then complain that it doesn't work.

Sometimes managers do the whole job so casually that it's hard to notice that they have done anything approaching performance appraisal. In employee surveys it is fairly common for people to report that they are not receiving enough feedback on their job performance. Managers in the same companies report that they are doing performance appraisal regularly. What really seems to be happening is that the managers talk to people in such general terms that the employees don't realize that what seems like a casual conversation is supposed to be their "official" performance appraisal. In some instances the problem is not that performance appraisal has been tried and found wanting, but that it has never really been tried at all.

But let's not put all of the burden on the managers. Designers of performance appraisal systems have made many of their own mistakes. Aside from the absence of training, they have frequently introduced systems without consulting the managers who would have to use them. Then managers see the systems as something imposed on them by an outsider unfamiliar with their day-to-day problems.

Managers are often advised to take a "kind" or "constructive" approach, especially where the feedback they have to give is negative. They see this as a requirement to go easy on an issue that their instincts tell them requires a tough approach. Another common complaint is that the systems are cumbersome. Many of them seem designed to produce completed forms to be put in files, rather than to plan and control the activities of an individual. Some systems fail in the other direction. They are simplistic, asking a manager to use check boxes to evaluate complex work.

Specialists in the field have also failed. They suggest that performance appraisal can accomplish too many things and offer it as a panacea. Then managements look for delivery on those promises. They expect the new system not only to accomplish the job of planning and control but also to be a source of information for salary administration, promotion, training and development, personnel planning, and documentation if someone is fired. In one of my corporate personnel jobs, we even used the performance appraisal forms to validate employment tests.

Properly applied, performance appraisal is a powerful tool, but it cannot do everything. If we limit its objectives, we can come up with a process that accomplishes its goals. This book takes a stand on this issue. The method of performance planning and appraisal you will learn from this book is designed primarily to help you and your employee plan, evaluate, and, if necessary, correct the employee's performance. In other words, the method should improve the employee's productivity and overall job performance, and it should help establish or enhance a relationship of trust, understanding, and cooperation between you and your subordinate. The administrative uses of performance appraisal—like salary decisions—may also be served by this process, but I will treat them as secondary.

If your company already has a performance appraisal system that you consider inadequate or too all-encompassing, don't despair. This book can help you too. Once you understand the system I am proposing, you will learn how to mesh it with whatever system your company employs. The next chapter gives you an overview of the goals of performance appraisal, and the reasons for doing it. I hope that chapter will serve both as a philosophical basis for your thinking and as a motivator to get you to apply this process. Then Chapter 3 gives you the how-to's. Each chapter thereafter deals with a particular aspect of performance planning appraisal and contains practical advice for making the experience a comfortable and productive one. Those how-to chapters also contain examples that can serve as models or dos and don'ts to guide you. Finally, each one has a summary you can use when you actually do one of the steps in the process; you can quickly refresh your memory on the important points. That way you can read the book and use it as a training aid to begin with and as a reference tool later. Okay, first let's tackle a little theory. (I promise not to overdo it.) I'll give you just enough to make sure you understand the why's of the things you have to do.

Remember: Performance planning and appraisal is not just another thing you have to do as part of your job as a manager. You can use the method described here as a way of carrying out your responsibility systematically.

Summary

- Performance appraisal is unpopular, but it isn't going to go away.
- Corporations use performance appraisal systems for a variety of planning and administrative purposes.
- Managers object to performance appraisal because:
  - It takes a lot of time.
  - It embarrasses them to sit in judgment of others.
  - It ruins any rapport they have with their subordinates, if it is done badly.
  - It requires training that they often don't get.
  - It often doesn't mesh with their managerial style.
- But managers often shortchange the process and then blame the system.
- Systems sometimes fail because:
  - They are designed by "experts" without input from managers who will use them.
  - They are cumbersome, with complicated forms to fill out and file.
  - They are simplistic, describing the complex communication needed to do a job in a phrase such as "gets along well with others."
  - They are implemented by executive fiat without the training or explanation required.
  - They are offered as a panacea by performance appraisal designers.
- This book emphasizes performance appraisal as a tool for planning and control.

Chapter 2

Purposes of Performance Planning and Appraisal

Performance appraisal involves the employee, the manager or supervisor, and the larger organizational unit. Each has objectives or hopes for what performance appraisal will accomplish. In many organizations performance appraisal is the basis for other personnel programs, like counseling, salary administration, or personnel planning. Sometimes it is the only formal program of communication between boss and subordinate required by a company. Very often corporate personnel people will try to design a system to do too much. In selling the idea to management, they promise that it will solve many problems and that it will provide data for several different kinds of decisions. There are many possible uses for performance appraisal, but a wise user of the technique will choose among the possibilities and confine performance appraisal to those activities that will meet limited, specific goals.

Performance Planning and the Corporate Planning Cycle

Corporations often institute formal performance appraisal systems as a means of translating their overall goals through the organization to the managers and individual contributors who will do the work to achieve the corporation's goals. For instance, if a company's strategic plan calls for the introduction of three new products over the next two years, many people in the organization will have to work on getting the products to market. Research, marketing, production, distribution—almost every function will have to be involved in some way. These efforts must be coordinated so that work duplication is minimized and still nothing falls between the cracks. Companies use formal performance planning and appraisal systems to reach such goals. The overall objective is set in the strategic plan, and then the activities involved in reaching the goal are broken down and assigned to the various functions. Each department takes its goals and breaks them down further by work unit until each person has a specific job to do to make sure the products get to market on schedule. In performance planning meetings these individual objectives are communicated to the people who will carry them out. This is the beginning of the performance planning and appraisal cycle. In practice it isn't that neat and tidy, but that is the theory, and a very sensible one it is. It provides a vehicle for organizing hundreds, or even thousands, of people toward a common goal.

Performance Appraisal and Salary Review

Regardless of whether the company uses the formal performance planning and appraisal cycle to organize and communicate the job to be done, most organizations that have a system use it to decide who gets a raise and how much. During the performance appraisal cycle, the manager documents the appraisal, usually on a form designed for this purpose. The information on the form is then used to divide up the salary pie. Often people are given an overall rating that determines how much of a raise they will get. Many organizations have elaborate formulas for figuring all this out.

The relationship between performance appraisal and salary review is controversial. Clearly, if the organization's objective in doing performance appraisal is to get information on which to base salary decisions, then salary will always be a part of the performance appraisal equation. There are some drawbacks to this, however. When salary and performance are discussed together, some employees may listen to the part about their salaries and not pay enough attention to the discussion of their performance. If salary is discussed first, they may spend the rest of the meeting thinking about how they're going to spend their raise and give little credence to the boss's ideas on how they can improve. ("If I'm really doing that badly, why did he give me a raise?") Or, if no raise is given, they may listen to their own anger or defenses instead of to the boss. ("Harry got a raise, and his work is no better than mine. I guess it pays to butter up the boss.") Some managers try to avoid this by talking about performance first. This tactic doesn't always work. If employees know that salary will be discussed at the meeting, they may not take the discussion of performance to heart. Instead they may weigh each comment to see if it means they will get a raise or not and get impatient waiting for the big news. ("Why doesn't she get on with it; who cares about all this stuff that happened eight months ago? I want to know how much I'm getting.")

There are other dangers to discussing performance at the same time that you communicate salary decisions. For one thing, far too often managers decide on a raise and then write a performance appraisal that matches the raise. In such a case, the performance appraisal doesn't make sense to the employee, and perhaps the raise doesn't make sense either. Some managers, knowing that the person's raise will depend on the appraisal, will be lenient to avoid conflict with the employee or because they want to give the person the "benefit of the doubt."

In most companies, a direct and explicit tie-in between performance appraisal and the amount of salary increase seems absent. Sometimes there are good reasons for the discrepancy—to keep salaries competitive, managers give "higher than merited" raises. Sometimes the reasons are capricious and arbitrary—for instance, for years women, regardless of their levels of performance, have been given lower raises because the myth is that "they don't need money; they have husbands to support them." If a company purported to have a merit increase system and there were no relationship between salary increases and performance appraisal, managers and employees would be quick to notice and criticize the discrepancy. There should be a relationship between the two, but most experts agree that they should be discussed separately.

Here's what the sequence should be. In one meeting the boss and subordinate discuss the plan they prepared and appraise the accomplishments. They both have a chance to feed their ideas into the discussion. They end by planning the employee's work for the next year. Then the boss makes salary recommendations after learning the employee's side of the story. This saves the embarrassment of later finding out something that should have influenced the fait accompli. (The decision usually has to be approved by the next level of management and perhaps by personnel.) When approvals are received, the manager communicates the amount of the raise to the employee and reaffirms their commitment to the work ahead. The first meeting should take some time; the second can be brief.

Performance Appraisal and Promotion Opportunities

These days most large organizations have job posting programs, where jobs to be filled are "advertised" within the organization and employees can apply for them. Appraisal information in the file is often used to assess an employee's readiness for a higher-level position. This doesn't cause too much mischief if the promotion is within the same group. Unscrupulous managers, however, have been known to give low ratings or bad recommendations to good employees who ask for a transfer or bid on a job in another area. These bosses do this so they won't lose good workers. The tactic usually backfires. The employees realize what's going on and leave, even if it means leaving the company. The supervisors lose the good employees they had hoped to keep and often gain a bad reputation by this kind of underhanded behavior. Capable, ambitious employees will not work for managers who hold good people back.

Companies also use performance appraisal information to make decisions about retention and firing. When staff cuts occur or are expected, managers sometimes inflate appraisals to protect their employees from the ax. This is one of the many issues clouding the accuracy of the information put on performance appraisal forms. Performance appraisal forms are also used as documentation when a person is fired. Many a performance appraisal form has been examined by a court or a human rights committee when a discharged employee has filed a discrimination charge. Clear documentation of marginal performance is necessary, and performance appraisals are considered one of the best ways to gather such information.

Performance Appraisal and Training Needs Analysis

Some organizations use performance appraisal as a source for analyzing training needs. Skill weaknesses or development needs are entered on the performance appraisal form or noted in the manager's assessment memo. Training managers then use these forms to determine what kinds of courses the company should offer and who should attend them. Even if the company does not have a formal program for assessing such needs, individual managers often find that training programs can be used to help an employee overcome a performance deficiency. So when a need to improve is discovered during performance appraisal, the manager looks for a program to help the employee overcome the problem.

Other Uses for Performance Appraisal

Some organizations use performance appraisal information as input to personnel plans. The most likely personnel planning application is to use the information to select high-potential employees who will be developed to take over top management positions. During the early 1970s, when the government began to require companies to validate employment tests, many personnel departments turned to performance appraisals for the information they needed to run their validation studies. If a high mark on the test correlated with a high performance rating, the test was considered valid. Since then, performance appraisals themselves have been challenged in court. In a later chapter we will look into the subject of the legal aspects of performance appraisal.

Clearly, organizations have asked a great deal of performance appraisal. As powerful a tool as it is, no one system can be designed to do all these things perfectly. By limiting its goals, we will strengthen, not weaken, performance appraisal. Managers and organizations need to choose what they will ask performance appraisal to do. This book deals with a system that directly benefits the manager and the employee rather than one that concentrates on gathering information for making personnel decisions. There are good reasons for this decision. First, organizations need effective ways to ensure that their "human resources," their people, will be used effectively. We are wasting our people's time and energy. We do this especially by not letting them know specifically what we want them to do. We wait until it's too late to tell them that they haven't done the job. We need to cut this out. Second, employees need humane treatment. A big step in that direction would be to give them a clear indication of what we expect them to do long before we judge how well they do it. They need feedback. They deserve to hear clearly and directly from us what we think of their work. Besides, if we make performance appraisal's primary goal that of administrative decision making, the process can always be subverted, appraisals faked to fit the decisions already made. We need ways of making personnel decisions, but we have a more critical need to plan and control work for high productivity and efficiency. If it is done well, performance appraisal can accomplish those goals.

What's in It for You?

Performance appraisal is a powerful mechanism for management control. Managers need ways of making sure that the work gets done well and on time. This means that managers need a systematic way of communicating their expectations to subordinates and of following up during and after the job. "Systematic" is an important word in that sentence. A manager's life is hectic—full of brief encounters with bosses, peers, and subordinates. Life in the plant, the office, the agency, or the hospital is fragmented by interruptions and crises. These conditions make performance appraisal more difficult since it requires continuity and some quiet periods for analysis and communication. But the very conditions that make performance appraisal more difficult make it absolutely necessary. The more hectic a manager's life and the more fragmented the time, the more necessary it is to have a system for communicating and evaluating what needs to be done. Otherwise these critical aspects of managing can get short shrift or be forgotten entirely. When that happens, no matter what managers do with their time, they are no longer managing.

Many managers complain of the stress they feel from their jobs. Often this stress is a result of feeling that things are out of control. Some managers don't sense the lack of control even when things are not as buttoned up as they should be. They go along blithely thinking all is well until a crisis occurs. Then they feel let down by their subordinates, who knew all along that disaster was approaching but felt helpless or uninclined to do anything about it. Managers need to keep on top of things, and performance planning and appraisal can provide the forum for the discussions with their subordinates that are necessary to keep the work under control. At the beginning of the cycle these manager-employee communications center on expectations and planning; along the way toward the goals and objectives, the system provides checkpoints for both parties to make sure the work is on track; at the end of a project or period, there is an evaluation; and then the cycle begins again with planning. This cycle can give the manager a sense of security—a feeling of being in control of the work that needs to be done.

Some managers try to gain this sense of security by false methods of control. They try to control the people instead of controlling the work. They do this through engendering fear with threats of reprisals, firing, and the like. Or they overcontrol their own activities with checklists and tight schedules and ignore the work or needs of their subordinates.

Some managers check everything everyone does; many try to do all the critical things themselves. There are many mistakes that managers make in pursuit of this feeling of security and control. But false security is shortlived, since repeated crises and the losses we suffer because of them destroy the feeling of well-being we desire and the good impression we hope to make as managers. We need real control and that means planning, follow-up, and evaluation for our sakes as well as for the company and the employee.

Many studies have been done on how appraisal affects employee motivation and productivity, and they are not conclusive. So many variables enter into things like productivity and morale that it is hard to get "clean" data for a study. However, most results point to a strong role for performance feedback. By giving employees information about their performance, you increase their ability to learn, help them maintain their level of motivation, and improve job performance.

Many managers, lacking training and information to help them make performance appraisal productive, have experienced the harm it can do if it's done badly. They fear it will ruin whatever relationship they have built up with their people. If the relationship is already strong, performance appraisal can enhance it. If the relationship is weak, the constructive discussions required by the planning-appraisal cycle can strengthen it.

As a manager, you get appraised too. The trend has been toward evaluating managers on their ability to sustain productivity and to counsel and develop their people. You score points with your boss if you have a systematic way of doing this.

There Are Problems for Managers

We talked about problems for managers in the last chapter—the time involved, the discomfort of judging people, the continuity and participation needed for performance planning and appraisal as opposed to the day-to-day way of doing business for most managers. These problems are real, and they won't go away just by naming them. Performance planning and appraisal require us to think, to analyze, to make difficult decisions. Talking to low performers about their performance problems can be embarrassing. It would be so much easier to just score them up a few points and ignore the issue.

We have also said that there are problems posed by overly complex performance appraisal systems that are cumbersome, or simplistic systems that are asked to do more and more. Sometimes our biggest problem is a boss who doesn't support the idea of planning and appraisal. Oh we may hear the boss talk about supporting it, but when it comes to devoting the time and energy needed we may feel we aren't being backed up. I have no easy answers for these problems. A former colleague of mine, Earl Garris, gave me an idea to remember. We had just left a staff meeting at which our fellow managers had complained bitterly about the difficulties of managing. After two and a half hours of "woe is us," Earl's response was this. "What those crybabies don't realize is that they're lucky management is hard. If it were easy, they could get anyone to do it. They wouldn't have to find smart people and pay them more and give them more status."

What's in It for Employees?

Employees have a great deal to gain if their managers and supervisors are conscientious about performance planning and appraisal. First, they too need that feeling of security. They get it from knowing clearly what is expected of them, from having opportunities to discuss problems and get confirmation that they are doing things well, and, at the end of a job or a period, from evaluating and learning from what they have done.

Performance appraisal also satisfies another basic human need—the need for recognition. We all get satisfaction out of doing something well, but the psychological rewards of work increase when we know our efforts are admired and appreciated. Unfortunately, in many businesses the "no news is good news" rule applies. Managers and supervisors don't give their employees the recognition they need—the recognition that will enhance their satisfaction and which, by the way, will also reinforce their good performance and make them want to continue it. In times of budget cuts or economic recession, we may find we have little or no financial rewards to give our people. Recognition takes on added importance in such situations.

For performance appraisal to reap these benefits for employees, however, it must be based on a system employees can trust. If employees feel that the feedback is coming from a person they cannot trust or if it seems to be based on whether the manager likes or dislikes the employee, it won't have the good effects we hope for. Feedback must also be given in a way employees can understand and accept. What good is feedback that is so vague that it is senseless? I once did a study for a major bank on the high turnover among its "high-potential" middle managers. One manager slotted on the replacement tables to be the next trust department head told me this story. His desk was in an area called in those days the "platform." What that means is that it was not in a private office but in an open, carpeted area with teak desks and potted palms, very conservative and quiet. The current department head's office was behind him. The department head was a short, bald man; his subordinates called him the gnome of Zurich. "One afternoon around three o'clock," the young vice president told me, "I was sitting at my desk looking over a customer's portfolio. I felt a little drowsy at that hour usually. All of a sudden, I felt a hand on my elbow and heard the gnome's voice whispering in my ear, 'There'll be an 18 percent raise in your next paycheck; keep up the good work.' By the time I turned around, all I could see was his back as he disappeared into his office. I wasn't sure until I got my next paycheck whether it had really happened or I had dreamed the whole thing." The bank this man worked for was wondering why so many "high-potential" people left when their prospects were so good. It was easy to find the answer; they didn't know how highly thought of they were. They got raises and promotions but no specific information and no concrete praise.

Employees at the other end of the spectrum have similar problems. If they are going to respond to exhortations to improve, they need specific information about what they should do differently. If the message is vague, the person may take the wrong action. For example, report writers who are told to make their reports longer usually just add unnecessary words.

New employees can learn a great deal from the performance planning and appraisal process: specifically what work they are to do, for and with whom they will do it, how well they are expected to do it, and what authority they have. All this can be clarified in the planning process. New or old employees can learn specifically what they will need to accomplish and by when, how they will be able to judge their own success, and what reports their managers will require.

The performance planning and appraisal system also gives employees a chance to think about, discuss, and plan for their own career growth. By getting accurate feedback on their present performance, they can maximize learning from the current job. A manager's opinion of their work will help them put their own strengths and weaknesses into perspective so they can choose a future career path realistically. In the planning cycle employees can let their managers know their aspirations and set learning objectives to help themselves prepare for their next career steps. They can also ask their managers for information about opportunities in the company.

The Need for Employee Participation

To make sure that employees realize the benefits and to ensure that they trust the system enough to respond to the information it gives them, it is best to involve them in the process from beginning to end. Just as managers resent performance appraisal systems foisted on them by personnel departments who never ask them what would be helpful, employees are likely to reject performance plans or appraisals that are made by their bosses and handed down to them. Too many managers think of plans and appraisals as something to write, not as a process that involves the subordinate. Yes, the results of the process must be written down, but that comes last. The thinking and the talking have to come before the plan or the appraisal is written.

These days we can assume that employees will expect, and sometimes demand, to be involved in planning their own work and in appraising how well they have done. If we want modern workers to be more productive, we must recognize that they, being better educated, will not easily accept authoritarian management. They aren't going to tolerate what their mothers or grandfathers expected in the workplace. They know what they want to put into the job and what they want to get out of it. This is true especially of technical and professional employees, but it is increasingly true of everyone—managers, nurses, workers on the line. Participation in the decisions that affect their jobs is coming to be seen as a right of workers. Employees can participate in all the phases of this decision making—helping to write their own job descriptions and objectives as well as helping to plan and evaluate their own work. Some organizations are even involving representative employees in the design of performance planning and appraisal systems.

If employees are involved in the planning and evaluation of the work, they are more likely to consider the appraisal and the system as fair. The process fosters teamwork between managers and subordinates, giving employees more of a sense of being "in on things." It is a way of combating that famous problem of worker alienation. Countless researchers have administered questionnaires to employees hoping to find out what contributes to job satisfaction. The list of needs employees hope to have filled in their jobs hasn't changed much over the years. Consistently, appreciation of work and feeling in on things come ahead of wages and working conditions.

The primary goals of performance planning and appraisal must be higher employee motivation and satisfaction. Employee involvement can increase the chances that these will be achieved. It is also interesting that when employees are involved in setting their own goals they are likely to set them higher than their managers would set them. And this in turn can lead to higher productivity and better performance.

On the other hand, those ubiquitous employee attitude surveys also tell us that performance appraisal may be as dissatisfying for the employee as it is difficult for the boss. Where the system is based entirely on the boss's subjective opinion and amounts to just a rating system, the employee may see it as unfair and unhelpful. After all, who wants to have someone sit down and check off boxes that say one's attitude is poor or that one doesn't get along well with others, especially when there are no specific instances cited when the employee did or didn't do what was called for. My friend Tom says he's waiting to see a form with "washes before he comes to work" on it.

These subjective rating systems do more harm than good. They also lead to some certifiable corporate insanity. For instance, suppose you work for Doug and he works for Ann. If Doug fills out a traditional rating form on you and rates you as "poor" in judgment, that form goes into your personnel file and stays there, sometimes indefinitely. But suppose that Ann, using the same form, rates Doug as having poor judgment. Does anyone go back to your form and write on it "this judgment was made by a person judged to have poor judgment"? No wonder employees often see the whole exercise as ridiculous or provoking. I once had a boss who rated me "average" overall. I had always thought of myself as "above average," perhaps even "outstanding." I was supposed to sign the form, but I refused to acknowledge that I was "average." (I was young then.) My boss threatened me with being fired for insubordination because I refused to sign the form. Not being ready for retirement, I signed it. Later he was fired for being incompetent as a manager, but the form remained in my file. I still get angry when I think about it.

In a performance appraisal system that begins with planning and involves the employee, there is little margin for this kind of problem. We are going to use a system that defines the job and clearly communicates expectations between boss and subordinate. Then subsequent appraisal can be based not on the employee's character or personality, not on what the person is—but on what he or she does. By beginning with clear definitions of what our employees must accomplish, how we expect them to do it and by when, we make the appraisal system into one that really appraises performance and not into an opportunity for character assassination. We will concentrate on what our people *do and don't do,* not on what they are or are not as people.

Summary

- Corporations use performance appraisal to:
  - Translate overall goals into objectives for individuals
  - Decide on salary increases and promotions
  - Document a decision to fire someone
  - Discover training needs
  - Assess potential as input for personnel plans
  - Validate employment procedures
- First, discuss performance with your employees, allowing them to feed in their own ideas. Later, recommend salary actions, and when they are approved, communicate them to the employees.
- Never give good employees a bad rating to keep them from being promoted to another department. You will drive good people out of the organization entirely if you do.
- Limit the goals of performance appraisal. Use it primarily as a tool to plan, control, and assess the work of your people.
- Use the performance planning and appraisal cycle to systematize your management work. You will gain:
  - Control of the work
  - Greater confidence
  - Relief from some of the stress you feel when things are out of control
  - Better relationships with your employees
  - Better performance appraisal from your boss

  Your employees will gain:
  - Clear knowledge of what's expected of them
  - Recognition for their efforts
  - A feeling of participation in decisions that affect them
  - Specific information on how they should improve
  - A realistic idea of their own strengths and weaknesses
- Involve your employees in performance planning and appraisal.
  - They need and want to have their voices heard.
  - They will be more likely to consider the system fair.
  - They will be more likely to demonstrate genuine commitment.
- Always base your appraisal on what the employee did or didn't do.
- Avoid assessing the employee's character or personality.

Chapter 3

Performance Planning

"If I had only known," Jake Barnes said to his wife the evening after his performance appraisal. Jake's appraisal had not been what he expected. When he went to meet with his boss to review his first year as bank branch manager, he felt satisfied with the job he had done. Things were under control. Turnover was down; his schedule for part-time tellers had substantially reduced the length of the rush hour line; with schedules organized, he had time to work with customers and solve problems.

Then at his appraisal interview he learned what his boss thought. She was happy with the new organization and praised Jake's skill in working with people. Everything he was proud of she admired—then came the "buts": He hadn't given high enough priority to marketing, his branch had one of the lowest increases in deposits in the region, his reports to her had been sparse, and he hadn't contributed enough at regional branch manager meetings. All this added up to an average rating for Jake. But Jake's problem was not that he didn't want to do what was required. Nor was it that he couldn't do it. It was that nobody ever told him what was required.

Studies show that only about one-fourth of all employees know what they will be evaluated on before the evaluation takes place. If they are going to respond positively to appraisals, employees need to know what yardstick is being used to measure them. Telling them what was right or wrong after the fact seems careless or, even worse, manipulative. You are told the rules after you've lost the game. *No fair.*

There is a lot of talk about making performance appraisal objective. This is a goal worth pursuing and many improvements have been made in that direction. For many jobs, however, total objectivity seems far-fetched. How do you objectively measure the output of cancer researchers? Do you count the number of journal articles they publish? On the other hand, most jobs can be defined well enough that the criteria for judging performance can be stated clearly, even if the performance cannot be measured objectively. The first step to really fair, believable performance appraisal is to define the job and the criteria by which we will judge performance.

Organizations as well as individuals will benefit from planning work more carefully and defining what is meant by good performance —not just making performance appraisal more reliable, but deciding what we really mean by productivity increase. Vague criteria not only harm employees, they hurt company performance. Some people don't contribute what they should because we haven't defined carefully what's needed; we can tell them about it after the fact, but the firm's dollars will have already been paid out for below standard performance.

As you will see when we discuss the legal aspects of performance appraisal, courts have challenged the lack of specific, valid criteria for making personnel decisions. To satisfy the need for validity, appraisal must be based on job-related criteria. Planning is the first step in developing such criteria. These legal requirements also make good business sense since having valid criteria means there is less room for error in managerial judgments. This increased accuracy should lead to better decisions as well as to more useful and believable feedback for employees.

At today's pace jobs are likely to change frequently. We can no longer tell a new employee, "Here are your duties," and go for several years without redefining the job. To keep pace with technology, gain productivity, and remain competitive, we have to redefine expectations from time to time. Performance planning affords us a systematic way of reviewing the viability of jobs and making adjustments before we fall too far behind.

More and more organizations emphasize planning, so even if we don't plan now, our managements are likely to demand it of us in the future. For you, the "future" may be now. You may already have to write plans for yourself and your people. You may moan, but think of the benefits:

- When we discuss goals with employees and they agree to meet them, those agreements become promises. Most people try harder if they've promised something.
- There will be fewer mistakes because employees will be given proper direction.
- We will have taken the time to think through what resources employees need to get the job done.

Basing performance appraisal on a plan, we turn appraisal into a process rather than an event. This process differs from old-fashioned rating systems most obviously in the amount of communication it requires between boss and subordinate. There is also room in the plan for personal goals as well as for work objectives and performance improvements. At performance planning time the manager and employee discuss and agree on the goals, duties, and standards for the employee's performance and set objectives for the work period.

How to Make a Performance Plan

According to the textbooks the first part of planning is to make the plans of the individual mesh with the plans of the company. Here's how it's supposed to work: Top management makes a plan for the organization, setting the direction of the company and deciding specific goals for the next period. Strategic plans are usually drawn up on a five-year-basis, and annual plans are based on the strategic plan. These plans are supposed to be specific and to ensure the prosperity of the company. Sometimes they actually do; sometimes they are poorly drawn and not very useful; sometimes they don't exist.

If your company is one that plans carefully, you probably have a corporate plan, a division plan, or the like. About 80 percent of the nation's largest corporations do set objectives, but the goals that these companies set are often financial and don't describe what is to be achieved to realize those financial goals. This goal setting is left up to department heads and managers, who sometimes complain about doing the planning. But it is their job. Every textbook says that managers plan, lead, organize, and control.

Goal setting as an organizationwide activity is also taking hold in many smaller firms and government agencies. Schools, hospitals and other organizations are beginning to see the virtues of careful planning. Chances are, then, that you will have some overall plan to use as the basis for your own group's plan. Needless to say, before you plan for or with your subordinates, you have to plan for yourself. If your organization doesn't plan formally, you may take an opportunity to ask your boss to work with you on your group's overall plan, pushing a little management development up the line as it were.

There is no plan unless it's written down. Unwritten plans, even if they are discussed, are amorphous and vague. Six or twelve months later people can't remember what they agreed to do, or they find out too late that they had different interpretations of what they committed themselves to do. So your first step is to write a plan for your group. Working with your boss, if possible, integrate your plan with the plans of the organization. You may want to get your own employees involved, perhaps in a group meeting. (How to do a thorough job of corporate planning is a subject for another book. The real subject here is planning the work of your subordinates.)

Once you have a plan for your group, you will use it as the basis for the individual's plan. Each employee will contribute to certain of the overall objectives. Some objectives will "belong" to only one employee. You begin an individual's plan by deciding which of the group's objectives the employee will work on.

I am about to suggest (very strongly) that you get your employees involved in planning their own work. But first some words of caution concerning your style as a manager. If your managerial style is more traditional, if you are more likely to make the decisions yourself, to tell people what's needed, and not to ask their opinions, then suddenly asking them to participate in planning may come as a shock. It may even make them suspicious of your intentions. If this is your style, you have two choices: one is to do most of the planning yourself; the other is, of course, to change your style.

If you do most of the planning yourself, your employees will be much less likely to accept enthusiastically your goals for them. You will also miss out on the value of their thinking and experience. But you will still benefit from having a written plan. They will understand clearly what is expected of them, they will spend their time working on what you think is important, and you will have criteria by which to judge their performance at appraisal time.

If you decide to change your style, you won't be able to do that overnight. But you can use the performance planning and appraisal process to begin to interact more with your employees, to show that you respect their knowledge and ideas. If you make a gradual transition to a different style of management, you may reap bonus benefits of more harmony and dedication on the part of your people.

Getting Your Employees Involved

To set realistic goals, it is essential that you get your employees involved, that you sit down with each person to concentrate on individual contribution. Experienced employees will be able to do this practically without guidance. Newer employees will need more input from you to formulate realistic goals and objectives. In either case it is better to plan with the employee. If you say, "Here's the job and here's how to do it," your employee will salute and say, "Yes." But that "yes" may not mean enthusiastic commitment. If you encourage open discussion, if you show you respect the person's intelligence and creativity, you are more likely to get cooperation. An employee who is involved will be less likely to feel resentful of work assigned, to see it as a punishment for past failures, or to feel singled out for extra work.

If you get the employee involved, you are more likely to base the plan on real job conditions. In the day-to-day crush it is easy to miss the small changes that take place in lead times or the capabilities of people in other departments who must contribute to the effort.

This employee involvement does not mean you forfeit your responsibility for planning and controlling the work of your group. Even though the employee may come up with the bulk of the objectives, may be able to plan the activities needed to achieve the goals, may correctly set priorities, and may even write up the plan, your role as a manager will be to guide the process and to approve the final result. Managers who lack confidence sometimes feel uncomfortable with this, preferring to be more directive, but as you develop your skill in managing, you will feel more comfortable sharing these tasks.

Once you get the employee involved, you must make sure that the person is prepared to do a good job of planning. It makes no sense to ask for opinions if the employee has no information on which to base an opinion. When you set up the planning meeting, give your employee as much information as is practical—goals and objectives set by management above your level, the job description, information about coming business conditions, new products or services coming down the line, budgets, and so forth. Later in this chapter you will get a checklist of information to cover.

When you meet with your employee keep the discussion open. Don't try to structure it too much. You want to foster creativity on both sides. Many managers and groups find a brainstorming session is useful to elicit ideas about goals and how to accomplish them. Learn this technique. Remember that the key issue in fostering creativity is to suspend critical judgment and to keep asking for more ideas; then sort out the usable from the impractical. Use the checklists at the end of this chapter to judge whether a goal should be accepted, then go on to identify when it should be done and what resources are needed.

At the end of the meeting either you or your employee will write up the plan. The written document will confirm what both of you have agreed to do. Accepting the written agreement will be an outward sign of your mutual commitment to the goals, objectives, and timetables.

The Need for Specificity

Vague statements about what will be achieved are not goals or objectives. They are just vague statements. A manager of a supermarket may think improving customer relations is a good goal, but it is only a place to start the planning. Once she knows that that's the general direction, the real objective setting begins. What does it mean to improve customer relations? Does she want to reduce the number of customer complaints to no more than ten a week? Does she want to reduce waiting time on line to no more than 15 minutes at peak hours? If she tells her assistant managers to improve customer relations and leaves it at that, there will be trouble.

When discussing this subject in management training programs, I frequently play this game: I write on the chart paper, "Considerable progress will be made on the XYZ project in the next month." I ask one participant to play the role of the subordinate and one to play the role of the manager. Both secretly write the percentage of the project they think will be completed. Then they show what they have written to the group. To the "worker," "considerable progress" usually means about 15 percent, sometimes as high as 25 percent, but to the "boss" it's never less than 50 percent and usually about 80 or 90 percent. The gap between these expectations may be the source of later problems, not only with performance appraisal but with accomplishing work that must be done.

Let's return to the example of the supermarket for an illustration of what might happen. If on hearing that the manager wants to improve customer relations, the assistant manager starts to spend considerable amounts of time greeting and being friendly with customers, he may have less time for training cashiers or making an efficient restocking schedule. Customer complaints about items missing from the shelves might increase and waiting time at rush hour might also increase. The subordinate will have spent time trying to meet his boss's objective, but the boss will see the situation deteriorating instead of improving.

Vague goals are practically useless. A good goal is specific, measurable, has a time limit, is realistic and challenging. A good performance plan contains such goals supported by action plans (the steps to be taken to achieve the goal) and a milestone chart (a list of interim deadlines and dates for follow-up meetings, and so on). The plan may even spell out exactly what authority the subordinate has to carry out the goal, what decisions the employee can make, how much money and other resources are available. The more complete the plan, the more likely it is to be achieved. And remember, if you don't write down the plan, it doesn't exist.

The Elements of a Good Plan

Let's go through each of the elements of a good plan.

Specific

This means the objective will state the work to be accomplished in terms that the boss and subordinate can *both* understand. When absolute specificity is impossible, you can at least set a range to guide your actions—between 10 and 15 percent, under $25,000, and so forth. Sometimes you will have to be arbitrarily specific. Guessing is okay if you can't do any better. As you work toward the goal, you will gain greater accuracy for the next time. If you have been vague, you won't learn as much.

Measurable

This means that the goal is quantified in some way. If you can write a goal that can be measured, you should. Many jobs lend themselves to this kind of scrutiny, but some don't, notably managerial and research work. In some instances, you may have to give up this criterion. But don't give it up too easily. Many managers find it difficult to write measurable goals because they haven't measured their group's performance. They can't say how many customer complaints a week would be an improvement, because they don't know how many they get now. It's something to think about. If measures depend on conditions, include the conditions as part of your plan. Then you can test your assumptions later on.

Time Limited

"Measurable" may be difficult to explain but "time limited" is easy. Put a time limit on every goal. Without a time limit a goal is a wish or a fantasy. "Someday" is what people say—"Someday we'll get the northwest region better organized," or "Someday I'm going to learn to give a decent speech," or "Someday my prince will come." If you put a date on it you're halfway to making it a goal.

Realistic

Some people tend to set goals beyond their reach. Your employees may do this because they want to impress you or because they don't have a realistic sense of their own limitations or the limitations of the job. You have to be careful of wishful thinking too. In an effort to get the most out of their employees, some managers set goals that are just too much for their people to handle; some managers even think this is a good idea. They feel it maximizes effort. It doesn't. Most people, when faced with a clearly unattainable goal, get discouraged and depressed and don't try at all. When it comes to goals, there's a buzz word for realistic: "doable," and it's a good one.

Challenging

We want realistic goals, but they shouldn't be too easy. "Ho hum" work doesn't excite people. Some managers and employees are tempted to set only easy goals so they will never have to admit that they didn't achieve them. This is true especially when they know they will have to file the plan with the boss's boss or the personnel department, when later decisions will be made on the basis of whether the goals are achieved, and especially when people might get fired for not meeting standards. But it is important for us to challenge ourselves and our subordinates. The "stretch" in the goal is essential if we want our people to reach new heights. Achieving a challenging goal is one of the most satisfying things a human being can do. This is real job satisfaction. If you are afraid someone else will punish your people for not achieving challenging goals, don't show your plan to anyone outside your own group.

Challenging goals are frequently the least easily defined. Often they are challenging because they break new ground, but for that very reason it is often difficult to make them specific and measurable. Especially in work like research, the truly innovative work is often the hardest to describe thoroughly ahead of time and the most difficult to evaluate. Unless we balance specificity and realism with real challenge and innovations, we will stagnate.

The better you understand your people, the better you will be able to guide them to the right balance between realistic and challenging goals. New employees, those who have had recent failures, or those who lack confidence should start with a little less challenge. Later they can build confidence from their successes and take on more. Confident, experienced people should be given their "wings." (Perhaps with a manager's safety net to make sure that no disaster occurs.)

Working Out the Plan

With these criteria as a background, let's turn our attention to actually drawing up the plan. Here are the action steps:

1. Begin with corporate or department goals.
2. Look at the employee's job.
3. Look at the employee's strengths and limits.
4. Consider the environment in which the employee will work.
5. Consider what managerial support the employee will need.
6. Draw up action plans.

Throughout this process your bywords will be to *set your people up to succeed.* If they do, you will too. So you will start with broad areas and limit them to what is manageable but still challenging, always keeping an eye on the priorities, making sure that you devote yourself to work that has a real payoff for the organization. Avoid the routine busywork that doesn't profit the company or the department in any substantial way.

I am going to describe these procedures, assuming that unless you have a good reason to leave your employee out of the process you will be doing these steps together.

Examine the goals of the organization. Imagine ways your employee can contribute directly to those goals. For instance, if the corporate goal is to increase sales by 17 percent, a district sales manager might have as a goal to increase sales in the territory by a like amount.

Another area to explore is how the employee can contribute indirectly to the organization's goals. Projects that improve administrative efficiency fall under this category. For instance, as a contribution to the sales increase goal, a computer systems analyst may cut down the firm's order processing time by two days. This doesn't directly increase sales, but faster order processing may give the firm a competitive edge and therefore indirectly affect sales.

Next take a look at the employee's job itself. Use the job description or last year's objectives and plan the ongoing or routine work that must be accomplished. The temptation will be to do this first and look at the organizational goals later on with the notion that we really ask ourselves, "After completing the routine work, what special projects can this employee undertake?" The fact is that the routine work may not be critical to the realization of the organization's goals. Concentrating on routine work involves us in the bureaucratic insanity found in so many places (where the clerk is filling out a request to have a light bulb changed, and the customers are walking out of the store because of the lack of attention). Current needs must take precedence over things we've always done and haven't recently evaluated.

The list of objectives or duties should be long and inclusive. Up to this point, you need to write down anything you can think of without regard to how possible it is. In other words, you brainstorm first. Then go over the list and assign priorities based on the value of the activities. I use the simple A-B-C method: Mark essential work A, important but not essential work B, and relatively unimportant work C. These designations will be useful as you begin to prune the list because of time, resource, and skill restraints. When you make tradeoffs, you will want to eliminate the C work first. In trying for the best plan, start from a broad range of options, then cut back.

Now you need to consider the capabilities of the employee. If the person is experienced and capable, you will have no trouble with this. Skilled and capable people can usually do it for themselves. New people need more guidance. Here the axiom about setting your employees up to succeed becomes essential. In considering the capabilities of new people, rely heavily on what they did on their previous jobs. Limit the amount of work, but don't give them busywork. The first days on a new job are times of high motivation for people. You cannot create that kind of motivation, but you can destroy it by not putting it to good use. The new employee still needs to have a little stretch. Make the objectives shorter term. People who have had recent failures also need the same kind of special consideration. Concentrate on the employee's strengths in choosing among the possible objectives.

For each objective, ask what new skills and knowledge a person would need to perform the work and compare these needs with what skills and knowledge the employee has or can develop either on the job as the work progresses or through training. The skills can be technical, communicational, analytical—anything down to how to operate a new piece of equipment. Filling in gaps in knowledge or skill can become part of the employee's personal growth objectives. If the gap is too broad to be filled readily, you may have to modify the objectives or assign them to someone else. Filling the gap may also lead to things for your own "to-do" list: work you will have to do because the employee cannot or, more likely, coaching to help the employee learn to do the work.

When you consider your employee's capabilities, don't let your own attitudes get too much in the way. Managers and supervisors are often susceptible to psychological projection. If they are confident, they can be overly optimistic about what their people can do or how confident their people are. The opposite is also true. Timid managers may be overly cautious in evaluating the capabilities of their people. In avoiding risks of failure, they pass up opportunities for real success.

The balance here is tricky. It's like teaching a kid to ride a bike. If you let go too soon, the kid will fall and perhaps get hurt. If you hold on too tight, the kid will never learn to ride the bike. If there is no risk, there is no real gain.

Next, consider the environment in which the employee will work. Projects may fail (and so may people) not only because of internal failings but also because of external problems. Support systems may not function as they should and this will mean failure because of things outside your employee's control. So once you have a tentative set of objectives with priorities, you have to start to think about what the employee needs to do the work. There will be certain things that you will have to make sure the employee has: money, staff, equipment. These are normally part of the budgeting process, and most managers don't have any trouble thinking about them. One thing they do often forget though is the issue of authority to match the responsibility. The people who complain most often that they don't have enough authority are first-line supervisors. Without sufficient leeway in making and executing decisions, employees cannot perform to their fullest. Anticipate what spending or decision-making authority your employee needs and write it into the plan. If an employee is not ready to accept the authority, if you don't trust an employee's judgment on certain points, then neither is the person ready to take responsibility for the work. You can either give the person the training needed to accept the authority, or you can retain responsibility for the work. If you hang on to all the authority, it's not fair to hold the employee responsible.

Another factor to consider is: What support from others will the person need, either within or outside your group? If such support is needed you may have to arrange for your employee to get full cooperation. Sometimes this means you have to inform other employees of the requirement (make it part of their objectives); you may have to negotiate with other managers for the support your employee needs. Consider the knowledge and skills of those who will support your employee's work. If there are deficiencies, you will have to either get them corrected (when members of your own staff are involved) or adjust your idea of what's possible (when the knowledge and skill gaps lie outside your area of control).

Consider the political climate in which your employee will be working. Will everyone be cooperative? Are there sensitive issues? Are those whose cooperation is needed likely to be generous with their help or will they hold back because they see themselves in competition with the person who needs their aid? Again, your employee may need special preparation to deal with the political realities or you may need to lower your expectations because of the political climate.

Next think through any changes that may affect the work. You may need contingency plans for likely changes. Consider all the possible obstacles, but don't overdo it, especially with new people. You want them to be realistic about the path they take; you don't want the future to look too full of quicksand and alligators. They'll decide not to go.

One Last Look

Now you need to go over the whole plan once more to make sure that it meets the criteria set at the beginning. Is it specific, are the outcomes measurable (if that is possible), do you have time limits set, and is the amount of work you have planned possible in the time allotted? Are the goals realistic and still challenging? Most of all, is the job meaningful for the organization and for the employee?

At this point you are making one last check. This is important, but don't do it with a fine-tooth comb. Especially if your employee has had a substantial role in formulating the plan, you don't want to get so picky that you give the impression that you disapprove. A good craftsman knows when to call the job done.

This last overview should include contingency planning. Consider the possible ill effects of succeeding, the possible downstream effects of the work. This is especially true for project work where your employee is instituting change. Say what you will do to avoid, prevent, or compensate for these ill effects.

Next make up your own plan based on the support you will be giving your employee. Plan for interim meetings to go over progress. Some managers like to do this at regular intervals, say monthly or quarterly. Some review when a milestone has been reached. Some ask for written reports which they then discuss. We will cover the subject of these interim meetings more thoroughly in the next chapter.

When you arrange for distribution of reports, be sure that your employees will receive directly any reports that deal with their work. Workers on the line should receive productivity and reject reports. All too often reports go only to managers. You need to know how your people are doing but so do the people themselves.

The last step of the planning is to draw up action plans. Here is where you will certainly want your employee to be involved. For each objective you will want a schedule of things the person will do to reach the goal. The result of the six steps to the planning process will be a written document that will guide your employee and later be the basis of the performance appraisal. You will eventually appraise how well your employee carried out the plan.

Setting Performance
Improvement and Personal Growth Goals

Part of any employee's action plan should be some personal development. These objectives can be improvement of some skill or work habit, or they can be preparation for a next career step. Here it is best for you to guide, but not dictate to, the person. If there is a problem with the employee's performance, you might want to suggest a solution as a personal growth goal. The best way to begin is to point out the issue. Be careful not to make your remark sound like an attack; state the issue in work-related terms and in the most positive way. You can say, "Bob, you are lazy and are squandering your talent. You'd better start making better use of your time if you hope to get ahead around here." Or you can say, "Bob, I think it's time you started reaping the full benefit of your talents. I know there is more you can contribute. Perhaps there is a way we can help you make better use of your time." The second approach may not work every time, but the first one is almost guaranteed to draw a defensive response.

One way to handle personal growth objectives is to build them into the regular work plan; perhaps this is the best way. In other words, you and your employee set a work goal that will accomplish a task that needs doing, but will also give the employee the opportunity to develop some knowledge or skill. For instance, if you have a person who is reluctant to speak up at meetings and this is blocking future career steps or causing problems with the work, you can make sure the person has a project that requires reporting at meetings and give the person some training or counseling to overcome the problem.

Limit the number of performance improvement goals. You don't want people to spend most of their time on performance improvement instead of accomplishing the work. And no one can make a great many changes or learn several new skills all at once.

Make performance improvement goals changes in behavior—not changes in personality. Employers have no right to tell a person what kind of personality to have. Besides, changing someone's personality is not an easy thing. Some trained psychotherapists say it is impossible. If you have ever tried to change any aspect of your own personality, you know what this means. And you know it never works when other people decide you should change.

Changing behavior that is related to actual job requirements is a different matter. Such a change is a possible and legitimate performance improvement goal. You may not be able to force an earthy person to try to be elegant, but you can stop a manager from making romantic overtures to the staff.

When it comes to helping the employee prepare for future career steps, act cautiously. There are two possible pitfalls. One is that your encouragement will seem like a promise of a promotion. The other is that you will wind up making the person's career decisions. Encourage the employee to set goals—long-range and short-range—but also encourage the person to keep career options open. It's good to have goals, but if they are too rigid, the employee can become locked into one idea and not be able to recognize and take advantage of unforeseen opportunities.

Thinking about career goals is hard when things are not going well. If the employee has not been performing well, you really can't bring yourself to discuss career steps. It may be, however, that if you suggest performance improvement goals in the context of the person's present job and as a prerequisite for advancement, you may turn on motivation that had been dormant.

It is also difficult to discuss advancement when the organization is not doing well. If the present situation is bad, we tend to think there will be no career opportunities soon. But our employees still need goals and future rewards for good performance. As the "baby-boom" babies hit their career stride, we will see an increase in competition for middle and top management positions. At this writing, it looks as if we will never be able to deliver on the implied promise of an upwardly mobile career for everyone. We will have to learn ways to challenge people even if we cannot give them a promotion every couple of years or an express ticket to the executive suite. We also need to develop ways of rewarding people apart from the normal big raise or big promotion syndrome.

Developing Standards of Performance

Once you and your employee have committed to specific, measurable goals that are within the employee's capabilities, turn your attention to standards of performance. This is really your job and your decision. Some managers involve their employees in discussing what those measures will be, but it is up to you, the boss, to make the final decision. Certainly, if you get your employees' opinions on this, you will have the benefit of their thinking on a topic they really know quite a bit about. And they are more likely to regard standards developed with their input as fair.

Developing performance standards is where managers who want to "get tough" can do so. High standards, provided they are fair and applied equally to all, actually seem to be the best. As is possible with putting some challenge in the work plan, we can bring out the motivation of our people by challenging them to meet high standards.

For some work, it is easy to set measures of performance. If you are managing a production line that makes alarm clocks, you can use the reject rate as a measure of performance. You can set a range: x number of rejects is unacceptable, y is average, z is good, and so on. This sort of thing is much more difficult with staff work and may be impossible with managerial work. Some people go too far trying to measure performance and lose sight of the mission of their group. As a training consultant I have seen management and professional development departments in large corporations measure their performance by the number of "person-days" of training. In other words, they get "points" for the amount of time the employees spend in training sessions without regard to the quality of the sessions. Does the fact that a manager sits in a conference room for three days at a program on presentation skills necessarily mean that his next speech will be a better one? Not according to me. There are useful measures of performance for most jobs. We have to make sure we don't adopt the facile ones just to save the time it would take to develop the more useful ones.

For managerial and professional employees you may have to develop a combination of objective measures of performance (like turnover rate or number of court cases argued) and some subjective standards. If you are going to subjectively evaluate your employee's performance, that is, base an evaluation on how you *feel* things are going, then you should describe as clearly as possible what you like and dislike, what you will observe, and how you are likely to react to these observations. This is not ideal, of course, but when more objective measures are impossible, this may be the only way. As long as your measures or way of judging performance are not mysterious, as long as you bring them out in the open, you should be able to maintain an atmosphere of fairness and cooperation.

If you are going to claim to pay employees for performance, you will have to find some way of relating your measures of performance to salary. Some organizations do this directly by having a system (either numerical or some other type) that dictates percentage of raise. For instance, some companies that use a management by objective (MBO) system relate salary to the meeting of objectives. Here is a basic continuum:

- Exceeds Most
- Exceeds Some
- Meets All
- Meets Most
- Meets Some

The basic rating, Meets All, means a person has met all the performance objectives; it corresponds to an average rating. It is impossible to get a higher rating unless the person's performance is at least at this level. Those who do not are rated Meets Most or Meets Some. (These ratings are considered okay if a person is new, the job has recently changed drastically, or there are other mitigating circumstances. But employees cannot get these ratings more than once without jeopardizing their positions.) Above the Meets All category are Exceeds Some and Exceeds Most. Of course, it's also possible for an extraordinary person to exceed all objectives or to meet no objectives. The former hardly ever happens if the objectives are set with the proper amount of stretch; promotions or extraordinary raises may be given in such cases. The latter, the Meets None performer, may be on the way out. Certainly, the manager would need to take serious steps to correct the problem—either the person is in the wrong job, the planning was entirely inept, or the employee has some serious personal problem.

Some organizations use a 1 to 5 rating scale. If your organization does, it is best to explain to your employees how you will arrive at the rating based on whether they meet or exceed the performance plan.

Whatever the overall rating system will be (if one must be arrived at), *make sure your employees know what it is.* You may sabotage all your efforts at productive performance planning and appraisal if a connection between performance and salary increase is promised but not there.

How Often to Plan

How often you will go through the planning, appraisal, and replanning cycle will depend on the nature of the employee's work, the amount of experience the person has, how confident the employee is, and whether the person's performance has been bad, good, or indifferent. Most managers work through the cycle at least once a year, but you may have to do it more frequently for some people.

A person who is working on projects of relatively short duration or one who works in an area where it is hard to predict even near-future demands will need to have appraisal and replanning more frequently, perhaps once a calendar quarter until things settle down. (Of course, you would not take salary action so frequently. We are talking here about planning and sticking to our guns about where the emphasis needs to be—on planning and control rather than on administration.)

A new person, especially one new to the company, will need more frequent planning sessions and more frequent interim follow-up. More experienced people will still need attention, but not as frequently.

A person who lacks confidence will need more frequent planning and follow-up sessions. This is sometimes a function of the person being new on the job, or a need for more support and encouragement may be just a part of the person's personality.

Employees whose work has not been satisfactory will also need frequent planning and counseling. If you are trying to improve the person's performance you may want to plan and review as often as once a month until the person is on track. More about this later when we discuss performance problems. Again, don't forget to give attention to your average and high performers as well.

In deciding how often to plan and review work, consider any special temporary needs your employee might have. For instance, when the work situation is pressured because of some problem outside the employee's control—unusually high volume, new methods or systems being installed, or complex technical problems—the extra support gained from frequent planning and review will be very helpful. Unusual pressures outside of work also make a difference. Family problems and health problems may mean your support is needed to see the employee through.

Regardless of what company policy may say about how frequently salaries are reviewed, you will want to gear the timing of your planning and performance appraisals to the needs of your people and your operation.

Your Attitude

Whether or not your employees are enthusiastic about the plan you make together will depend on many things, not the least of which is your own attitude toward the work. When you, as a manager, are energetic and positive, when you project an image of commitment and diligence, that enthusiasm can be contagious. Your people will see you not only as their manager but as one whose attitudes and actions have been rewarded by the organization. What they see you do, the image you project, will seem to them to be what is required. If you work hard, if you are enthusiastic, if you create an atmosphere of fairness and commitment, if you seem to enjoy your work and care whether they enjoy theirs, they will respond with their own enthusiasm and commitment.

There isn't much else to say on this issue, but please don't believe that because it doesn't take up too much space it isn't very important. It is critical. You may do everything by this and every other book and still get it all wrong. If you can't show enthusiasm because you don't feel it for your own job, learn what's wrong and deal with it. If you just don't like management, go into another field. A chemist who doesn't like being a chemist affects only herself. A manager who is indifferent drains energy from the entire group.

Potential Problems

In thinking about undertaking any activity it's best to know where the pitfalls are. With performance planning and appraisal there are many.

The major one for planning is that there is a tendency to avoid it altogether. There are a great many excuses for not planning. People who avoid planning also find it very convenient to avoid appraising. And if they haven't planned I don't blame them for not appraising. Without a plan to use as a yardstick, it isn't possible to appraise performance. As my friend Rick Piper once described it, that game is, "Shoot the gun first; then we'll hold up the target." Without planning, appraisal degenerates into character assessment, which makes most managers nervous and most employees defensive. The issue is that we must plan, but we often avoid doing it. Why? For a ton of reasons.

First of all, the planning and appraisal cycle is usually an idea introduced by the personnel department. Regardless of its level of competency, personnel (or, as it is now widely known, human resources) is not a function that always commands a great deal of respect in an organization. If performance planning and appraisal is seen as "just another personnel department program," managers and employees may prejudge it as being useless and not bother to try it.

People also avoid planning because they prefer to avoid the commitment it implies. If you write a plan, you feel you have to stick to it, and any aimless wandering around has to stop. I guess planning is not for lazy people. But I also believe that most people are not lazy. They work hard. Frequently their accomplishments are paltry compared with their efforts, and they feel frustrated. Planning can help solve this problem and make you feel more satisfied with your work. By planning we also make sure our organizations get their money's worth. We may pay people more than they are worth to us, and they may feel they are paid too little. At this writing, the American business community is screaming its head off about productivity, but individual managers still seem reluctant to define what productivity means.

Those definitions, I must admit, can become political footballs. If you write a plan, it can be scrutinized; your boss can disagree with it or accept it as a promise to accomplish everything you wrote down. Since a first attempt at planning isn't likely to be all that accurate, you may feel a little apprehensive about doing it if your boss is likely to be harsh when it comes to evaluating the plan. But don't give up on planning. Make a plan, and if the political climate in your organization doesn't foster the idea, just don't show it to anybody.

Another pitfall is to make plans that are so vague as to be useless. This may also be the result of the political atmosphere. If a plan is required but the organization somehow makes us fear planning, we may write a plan that is so vague it means nothing. If you're going to do that and call it planning, you might as well not bother. It's just a waste of time.

Some managers don't go far enough; others go too far. They push their people to agree to unrealistic goals. Or they themselves believe that more can be accomplished than is possible. This is a problem particularly for very ambitious managers. They want more from their people than their people are willing or able to give. They confuse leadership and challenge with coercion.

Managers who are themselves extraordinarily talented may make the mistake of setting unrealistic goals. First-line supervisors who have recently done their subordinates' job use what they perceive to have been their own level of performance as the standard for the work of their subordinates. This is dangerous for two reasons. First of all, the supervisor's level of contribution may have been extraordinary, beyond the reach of the average worker. Second, and perhaps more likely, the supervisor may not remember correctly what it was like to do the job, may not have an objective perception of what his own performance was like, or the conditions may have changed enough to make the job substantially different. One thing certainly has changed: the present incumbents have a different, new, and inexperienced supervisor.

Planning Group Work

Where the work will be done through team effort—several people working in concert to produce the product or effect—it is best to carry out the planning in group meetings. You use the same techniques and checklists developed for planning one-on-one; you just do it in a group setting. This can be a time-consuming process, especially if the group has not worked or planned together before. You will need to be careful to keep the meeting on track and to keep the group focused on the issues. But the extra time you spend will be worthwhile in the long run because your people will have an opportunity to work out ahead of time any difficulties they anticipate. It is especially useful in helping people avoid conflict as they work together. Group planning sessions allow them to work out what responsibility belongs to what person. This keeps the territorial issues to a minimum later on.

There are some side benefits to group planning. It fosters a feeling for the team, something we all know helps generate energy and enthusiasm. And it helps people develop their communication and group problem-solving skills.

Be careful that group planning doesn't turn into a gripe session. You will have to keep people from going off on "woe-is-us" tangents. The griping will most likely come up when you begin to go over the possible obstacles to getting the work done. Employees may begin to name human obstacles or problems with corporate policy, or another department's way of doing business. A certain amount of ventilation on these issues is actually good. Let them get the gripes off their chests. You will also learn about issues they face. You may have to go to bat for them to change a policy or negotiate better cooperation from other areas. But, you have to keep the lid on crybabyism. Keep asking questions like, "What can we do about that?" "If we can't change it, how can we get around that problem?" "How can we change our plan so that we set a goal we can accomplish despite the problem?" By raising these issues you will keep people thinking about the plan and how to make it workable. Your questions will also help them focus on actions they can take to solve their own problems instead of sitting around feeling bad because no one ever volunteered answers to questions they never asked.

Summary

- The first step to performance appraisal is to define the job and the criteria by which we will judge performance.
- Benefits of performance planning:
  - Employees are more likely to be committed to the work.
  - Employees will take fewer false steps if we set a clear course beforehand.
  - Employees will have the support and resources they need to get the job done.
- How to plan:
  - Always write your plans; don't just think about them.
  - Begin with overall organization or department goals.
  - Get your employees involved in the planning of their own work.
  - Set goals and plans based on overall organization objectives.
  - Add work described in the employee's job description.
  - Modify plan based on employee's strengths and limits.
  - Modify plan based on limits imposed by the environment in which the employee will work.
  - Make detailed action plan, including actions manager will take to support the employee's work.
- Brainstorming may help you and your employees broaden your thinking about what work to include in the plan.

- First, list everything you can think of regardless of whether it is practical.
- After you have listed all your ideas, prune the list to those that are most productive.

- Benefits of employee involvement in planning:
  - Their knowledge and perspective will make the plan more realistic.
  - They are more likely to commit to the plan with enthusiasm.
  - They are less likely to resent being assigned certain tasks if they know why they are doing them and how they fit into the larger picture.

- Criteria for a good plan:
  - Specific
  - Measurable
  - Time-limited
  - Realistic
  - Challenging

- Work plans should include not only objectives but also action plans and statements about the limits of an employee's authority.

- Don't forget to make your own action plan about what you must do to support the work and your follow-up dates.

- Include personal growth objectives in the plan. These can be:
  - Performance improvement goals
  - Career-related goals

- Set performance improvement goals that:
  - Relate to the work
  - Are built into the regular work plan, if possible
  - Represent changes in behavior not personality

- Career goals should be:
  - The employee's own
  - Flexible
  - Both long-range and short-range

- Set standards of performance high and apply them fairly and equally to all employees.

- Relate overall standards of performance to salary. A possible system is:
  - Exceeds Most
  - Exceeds Some
  - Meets All
  - Meets Most
  - Meets Some

- Your own enthusiasm for the plan sets the tone for the employee's response.

Checklist 1

Prepare the Employee to Plan

- Provide copies of organization or department goals.
- Ask the person to review the job description.
- Share information about future business conditions:

  Economic forecasts
  Sales forecasts
  Planned changes in product line, organization, or staffing

- If the budgets for the year have already been approved, share the budget as it affects the individual's work.

Checklist 2

What About the Special Employee?

New Employees
- Go a little light on challenge.
- Give them productive work right away.
- Make objectives shorter term.
- Concentrate on known skills and knowledge, things they've done in past assignments.

Poor Performers
- Accent realistic goals.
- Concentrate on their strengths.
- Plan more frequently.
- Plan for performance improvement over a reasonable period of time.

Timid Employees
- Accent realism in goals.
- Give them plenty of encouragement.
- Plan more frequently.

Experienced, Confident Performers
- Go high on challenge.
- Allow them to evaluate their own capabilities.
- Plan less frequently.
- Give more authority.

Checklist 3

Is the Plan a Good One?

For the Employee

- Can the person reasonably be expected to do the work?
  Have there been previous successes with similar work?
- Can the worker learn the required skills or gain the needed knowledge and keep up with the workload? Consider knowledge of the company, its products, its customers, and the employee's coworkers, as well as skills and technical information.

  What experiences, courses, coaching, and counseling will the employee need during the learning period?

- Will the plan sustain the interest and enthusiasm of the employee?
- Will the employee need support from you or others to complete the work?

  What arrangements can you make to remove potential obstacles?

- What limits do you want to put on the employee's authority to carry out the work?

In Your Environment

- Is there time to do the whole plan?
- Are there sufficient resources—people, equipment—to get the job done?
- What are the budgetary limits within which the work must be done?
- What difficulties will your employee encounter because of organization, work rules, personalities or experience levels of customers or coworkers?

  What can you do to remove such difficulties?
  What warnings and information will help your employee succeed despite the difficulties?

- What political issues impinge on the employee's work?

  Can the person handle these issues?
  Should you become involved in parts of the work?

- What changes in or outside the organization are likely to affect the work? Consider the economy, laws or rules, organization, personnel, product line, technology. Will priorities change?

What contingency plans do you need to make for uncertainties?

- What are the downstream effects of the work the employee will be doing?

  Can any potential problems be avoided by adjusting the plan or better preparing people for the changes that will occur as a result of the planned work?

Chapter 4

Interim Follow-Up

Once you have made a performance plan, you and your employee need to manage that plan. That means your employee must do the work as planned and you must keep the plan on track. By having a clear and specific plan,your employee can have most of the control over the work. But, you need to intervene at regular intervals. Let's talk about how.

Of course, you will observe and interact with your people fairly constantly, but part of your plan will be to schedule regular follow-up between the planning and the ultimate appraisal meetings. You and your employee will meet to review the progress made on the work plan, arrive at solutions to problems, and adjust the plan to better fit reality if that is necessary. This work is an essential part of the planning-appraisal process. In the first step, planning, you set your course. In the last step, appraisal, you review where you are and figure out if that is the place you expected to wind up. The middle step is for checking to make sure you are on course and to see if the final destination you chose still makes sense. You need to do this while there is still time to change direction or rescue the work if it has gotten off course.

Interim follow-up is also an opportunity for you to do, in a scheduled and more formal way, what you ought to be doing continuously: giving encouragement to the troops. Most bosses know they need to do this often, but the press of daily business makes it haphazard. Sometimes we think we do more of it than we really do. For instance, we could easily overlook the needs of the person whose projects are going well while we are problem solving with the person who is having big trouble. Both need attention, and you need a systematic way to make sure that they both get it. This is your opportunity to be a "cheerleader" for your people. You need to applaud their successes. And if they aren't making it, you need to cheer them on to try harder or smarter. And every plan, especially if it is challenging, contains some objectives that will not work out. You need to rework these to make them more realistic or eliminate them before they frustrate and distract your employees. This interim meeting will give your employees another opportunity to participate with you in problem solving and decision making. If you are going to try participative management, it won't work to do it once a year at performance appraisal time. Your people will want consistency in style. Besides, they will be suspicious of your request that they participate at appraisal time if that is the only time you ask them to meet with you to discuss how they are doing. In fact, they are likely to be suspicious of your whole appraisal if you speak to them about their work only in a formal meeting once a year.

Plan your interim follow-up meetings to be a positive, motivating force. This is particularly important for employees who are working on improving performance deficiencies. Keep interim meetings with them as encouraging as possible. Of course, if they aren't making the progress they should, you will have to tell them. But if they are improving, concentrate on congratulating them and being very specific about the improvements you see. Some managers are tempted to exhort people who have improved to keep trying by reminding them of the bad job they used to do or of the evils of lateness and so on. Forget that. If you used the preaching routine once and it worked, go on to something new.

Time spent at interim meetings can have a wonderful effect on the relationship between you and your employee. That relationship is important today and will grow to be critical in the future. More and more modern workers expect that their relationship with their bosses will be interactive and positive. Part of the reward they expect from the job is a feeling of achievement for a job well done. Your formal and informal discussions with them will be part of this reward system. It will also give your employees a steady diet of the confirmation and assurance we all need.

How steady should that diet be? That depends. In most organizations formal performance appraisal is required once a year. Where management by objective or some similar program has been installed, planning is usually done annually. But, certainly no one suggests that boss and subordinate speak together only once a year. How often you schedule more or less formal interim reviews will depend on the same factors we discussed when deciding how often to do planning.

The first thing to consider when deciding when to schedule an interim review is the needs of the employee's job. A chemist working on a six-month stability study doesn't need to review the project's progress every month. Choose a schedule that conforms to the work cycles, to the peaks and valleys of the workload, or to milestones in the life of the project. Certainly, you will want to review progress before a critical due date and far enough in advance so that the project can be rescued if you uncover a serious problem during the review. In this way you can keep control of the work without smothering the employee.

Meet with the employee and review your plan whenever there are serious changes in the work situation. If these can be anticipated (for instance, someone retiring), meet before the change to plan a smooth transition. If the change is unanticipated, meet as soon as possible after you notice it.

New employees, insecure employees, or employees with performance problems will need more frequent follow-up. For new people, you will want to review their initial training and planning frequently, perhaps even monthly. When a new person arrives, there is so much information to absorb that not all of it sinks in. Frequent reviews at the beginning can fill in the blanks left by the information overload of those first few days on the job. If you are going to make a mistake about the timing of interim follow-up, do it too frequently, rather than not frequently enough.

These meetings will serve as reassurance for you as well as for your employee. Therefore you should hold one whenever you need reassurance (provided you are not a bundle of insecurity or you may annoy your people or give them the feeling that you don't trust them). Invite your employees to schedule interim reviews with you any time they feel they need to go over progress and problems.

In the review meeting you want to make sure that the work is progressing and is indeed productive. Once people get involved in activity, they can sometimes begin to see being busy as rewarding. Eventually they will get an empty, useless feeling when they realize, as my brother Andy describes it, they have one foot nailed to the floor. Use the interim review meeting to keep people feeling productive.

Before the Interim Review Meeting

To prepare for the meeting, you and your subordinate should each review the progress of the work against the work plan. You should each be prepared to review the status of the work as you see it and to cover obstacles and problems and tentative ways of dealing with them. Some managers ask for all this in a written report before the meeting and then use the meeting time to discuss issues and reach agreement on a course of action. If you have been systematic about documenting your observations of the work as it progresses, you may have a file of source material for the discussion.

At the Interim Review Meeting

At the meeting ask your employee to review progress first or if you have gotten a written report make sure that you have properly understood its contents. If all or part of the work has been going well, congratulate and compliment your employee. Be specific about what you have liked. A statement like, "Good job so far, Jake," is not performance feedback. Spend some time talking about areas where you feel your employee faced some difficulty, say what you think the person did to succeed. These words will reinforce the behavior for the future. They will also help the person isolate which actions most contributed to the success so far.

What to Do if the Plan Has Gone off Track

In making the performance plan in the first place, what you have really done is to delegate the work. But you can delegate work and authority, you cannot delegate responsibility. To discharge your own responsibility you must make sure the work gets done well and on time. These interim review meetings will help you do that as well as help the employee keep up the necessary enthusiasm and energy. They will also contribute to your own sense of security and remove some of the stress you feel when you aren't sure things are in control.

Of course you will be observing how things are progressing fairly constantly. You will comment on small matters casually in your day-to-day conversations with your people. This is the best way to handle the trivia. If you save the minor details for a more formal meeting, you will come across as picky and insensitive. If it is important to you, by all means say you wish the daily activity log were kept a little more neatly. But if everything is there and it's legible, don't make a major statement about it. It's best to use a light touch—talk about how glad you are that it's up to date and make the other remark an aside. If the plan has gone off track, the first thing you have to do is to figure out why. Don't jump to conclusions and immediately blame the employee, even if it seems on the surface that the person just isn't doing what's required. There are many reasons why people don't succeed:

- They don't really understand what they should do.
- They don't know how to do it.
- They are prevented from doing it by the system.
- They are punished if they do it.
- They see no reward in doing it.
- They suffer no losses if they don't do it.
- They can't do it no matter how hard they try.

Each of these problems has a different solution. Lectures and exhortation are unlikely to work in any case. But until you know the reason for the lack of progress, there is no point in taking action. Discuss the matter thoroughly. Look for causes. Don't resort to blaming the employee. If the discussion seems to be turning into a witch hunt, you won't get much useful information. And information is exactly what you need to figure out what's really going on. Ask questions but be careful that they don't seem like accusations. Tell your employee that you are looking not to lay blame but to get to the root of the problem. Keep the reasons I've given you in mind and try to find out what the real cause is. Once you've isolated that, the solution should be fairly easy: a clearer explanation of what's required, some training in the skills required, a change in the system, or building into the system the proper rewards.

Some problems are trickier than others. Some managers find it difficult to believe that people can be punished for doing the "right" thing. It happens. When I was working my way through college, I got a summer job working for a firm that reevaluated real estate for tax purposes. The clerical staff in the temporary office were all women, mostly students or recent high school graduates who couldn't type and needed work. We computed the value of homes from information given on cards. Our supervisor was a woman not much older than we. She rang a little bell when we were to start and end the workday, and before and after breaks and lunch. For the first couple of days she taught us our work. Then she announced that we would be expected to complete 50 cards a day. That wasn't too hard; we could all do it. Then she raised the quota to 60 and 70. At 80 cards a day, Miriam started having trouble.

She was a sweet girl from a poor family. We all liked her, and she really needed the job. We would each take a few of her cards and get them done for her, but at that point we were all working at our limit. When the workload increased they hired two new people. By 10:45 on their first day of work, we told them that they should never finish more than 80 cards a day and that we would all like them better if they took their time getting to that level. I don't know what we would have done if they hadn't gone along with us; we would probably have just ostracized them. But performing at a higher level would definitely have been "punished." In fact, we would have felt punished if we had worked faster and Miriam had been fired because she couldn't keep up. Exhortations from our supervisor would have done no good, I'm sure. I didn't know I was learning about management then, but I was.

Employees who can't do the job no matter how hard they try present a different kind of problem. This problem is discussed in Chapter 7 in the section about dealing with poor performers.

If it becomes clear that the original plan is no longer viable, you will have to modify the plan to meet the situation and the time constraints you now face. Work out the new arrangement with your employee, renew your commitment, and start afresh. Avoid the trap of frustration, concentrate on what you can do to solve the problem. Let your employee talk out any discouragement. But don't either of you wallow in it.

It is easy, too, to feel discouraged about planning when the original plan fails. Be patient with yourself. Planning is a skill—like skiing or driving a car—you have to do it for some time before you get really good at it.

Write the changes you agree on, either in the plan or on a separate sheet. At this point you may also want to make some notes to refer to later when you are doing your periodic appraisal. While you are still thinking of them, write down the things you will want to remember for the next appraisal. And don't forget to write down the positives as well as the problems. Most managers don't spend concentrated periods of time with their employees unless there are problems. For this reason, we can get the impression that problems are the rule rather than the exception, even when this is far from the truth. You may need a file of notes to yourself to keep a balanced perspective.

You and your employee will come out of the interim review with things to do. You may have the longer list. Reorganizing and restructuring the environment may be necessary to make it possible for your employee to complete the work. You may need to meet with people from other departments to remove roadblocks that the employee can't deal with. You don't want to usurp the employee's responsibility or take away the growth opportunity or the feeling of accomplishment that comes from solving one's own problems. However, there are times when your status, clout, or personal contacts can smooth out a situation that the employee would find impossible or too time-consuming.

These interim reviews, like planning, can be carried out in groups. The problem-solving aspects may often be easier when there are more minds around to work on the issue. Some managers schedule periodic "minireviews" at staff meetings. They hold the normal one-to-one reviews, but each month they devote a staff meeting to reports from each person on how things are going and to mutual problem solving. This not only brings other minds to bear on the problems, it fosters a team spirit among the staff members and keeps them informed of one another's work.

Summary

- Interim follow-up allows you to:
  - Correct planning mistakes before it is too late.
  - Coach and counsel employees to keep the work on track.
  - Encourage progress.
  - Strengthen your relationship with your employees.
- How often you schedule interim meetings depends on:
  - The job—peaks and valleys and milestones inherent in the work
  - The employee—the person's experience, past record, level of confidence
  - Your need for information about progress
- Hold an interim review:
  - Well in advance of critical due dates
  - Whenever there is a serious change that affects the work
  - More frequently for new or insecure employees and for poor performers
  - Whenever you or your employees need assurance that things are on track
- To prepare for an interim review meeting, you and your subordinate should:
  - Review progress against the plan.
  - Analyze shortfalls.
  - Be ready with suggested action steps for solving problems.
- You may want to ask your employee for a written status report that you will discuss at the meeting.
- Give specific feedback; even if everything is going well, say why and how.
- Reasons the plan might have gone off track:
  - Employee doesn't understand it.
  - Employee lacks requisite skill.
  - The environment makes it impossible.
  - There is no reward.
  - Success leads to "punishment."
- If the plan has gone off track:
  - Figure out why.
  - Don't lay blame.
  - Work out a plan aimed at overcoming the problem.
- You may have to modify the original plan, based on what you find out during interim review.

Chapter 5

Preparing for
the Appraisal Interview

Preparing for a performance appraisal interview is like preparing for a trip. Sometimes you can just throw some things in a bag, set out, and have a really great time, but if you want to be sure to have a good time, you take the time to prepare.

Select the Proper Time and Place

Pick a time when you and your employee will be able to concentrate. Remember you are going not only to review past performance, but also to plan for the next period. The appraisal may take more than one meeting, but it should seem like one process and therefore be done within a few days. Both of you must be relatively free from distractions. There will probably never be a time when you are totally devoid of other problems, but at least avoid obviously bad times, like the moment when one employee is waiting to hear if she's got the mortgage on the house or when another's wife is about to give birth.

The timing, as we discussed in the chapter on planning, must make sense in terms of the work as well as in terms of the employee's experience and personal needs. Since you will be doing appraising and planning at the same time, all that applies to planning also applies to appraisal.

Geography is important. First of all you must ensure privacy. No one can concentrate on a discussion of performance if it takes place in a goldfish bowl. Absolutely no one should overhear the conversation. If there are important files in your office that people must get to or if you don't have a private office, reserve a conference room, borrow an office, find some private space. In a training session a manager once told me there was no private space at all where she worked. I suggested she go out in the parking lot and sit in a car. A ridiculous idea, but that's how strongly I feel about privacy.

Plan to hold the meeting in a place where you and your employee can sit face to face without a desk or table between you. If you sit behind your desk with your employee on the other side, you will represent an authority figure. This doesn't encourage a free flow of discussion. If you need a surface to write on as you plan, sit together on the same side of the table.

Some managers are sensitive about where the appraisal interview takes place. John Davis of Waters-Trego in Dallas gives his employees a choice: their offices, his office, or neutral territory. He says this issue only lasts for the first appraisal or two. Once the relationship is well established, no one seems to care where the meeting is held, as long as it's private.

Once you have selected the time and place, you will make the appointment with your employee. Do this well in advance of the meeting. The employee will want to come to the meeting prepared. In fact, later in the book preparing the employee to do a self-appraisal is discussed. There must be time to do this adequately. Once you have made the appointment, you must keep it. If you cancel or postpone it, you will be sending your employee a powerful message: that whatever you are going to do is more important than good performance. By all means don't cancel at the last minute. And never change the date and then change it again.

You will need to prepare your own appraisal of the employee's performance, and you will need to prepare your employee to make a self-appraisal. Let's start with your appraisal.

Assessing Your Employee's Performance

Planning your employee's work carefully will make this aspect of performance appraisal much easier, but no matter how carefully you have planned you still need to assess performance with great care. An appraisal is like most activities; if you aren't willing to put much effort into doing it, you aren't going to get much out of it. Some managers do the whole thing casually without much forethought. Then they expect great changes in their employees' behavior. They don't realize that employees respond, consciously or unconsciously, to the effort that bosses put in. Besides, no matter how carefully you scrutinized the plan at planning time, no matter how clever you were in assessing the future, when it arrives, the future tends to deal a few surprises.

Fairness dictates that you will do this part of your job carefully. We have said before that many managers detest performance appraisal because they feel so uncomfortable sitting in judgment of others. With our careful planning and employee involvement, we have tried to make the process as fair and objective as possible. This should make it seem less stressful for you since you will be judging the work not the person. But you may still feel uncomfortable. If you do, work harder rather than avoid the issue. I know that people tend to avoid things that make them uncomfortable, but if you give your assessment short shrift so you can get on with doing things that are more fun for you, you could do your organization and your employee a great disservice. The performance appraisal you write today will probably be in the employee's file for many years to come. Decisions will be made based on what it says; if the information is inaccurate it will hurt the employee and the firm. This is probably not comforting, but it is real.

The first step to doing a useful appraisal is to gather information. You will need to look at what the person has done over the review period. Go back to the plan to see how much of it has been accomplished. Look again at the employee's job description for the things that should have been done and compare them with the actual results. You may also have reports of such things as production or sales that will give you a picture of your employee's performance. If you have been following your schedule for interim coaching and counseling, you should have some notes in the file about how things have been going, about things that you found especially admirable or lacking in the employee's performance. Now is the time to pull these out. Remember, it isn't fair to start observing the employee's performance the week before the appraisal meeting and base all your judgments on what you see. You could be getting a skewed picture. For one thing, the week may not be a typical one; it may show the employee at either a disadvantage or an advantage compared with the regular course of work. Furthermore, the employee undoubtedly knows that performance appraisal time is near. That may make her nervous and cause her to work inefficiently or it may cause him to work extra hard to make a good impression. No matter how closely you work with people, you will not know everything they are doing. Now is the time to find out what you know and what you don't know and make up the difference.

You also need to make sure that you concentrate on important matters. Don't let your appraisal drift into minutiae; your employee won't take what you have to say seriously. Nor will your opinions be given attention if they are based on false assumptions. Make sure you are aware of any recent changes in the work environment or other factors that could have made the job easier or more difficult than you originally thought.

Pitfalls to Accurate Appraisal

It is also important that you be aware of difficulties that arise in making an assessment. These are problems that everyone runs into and knowing about them can help you avoid them.

First of all remember that some people have a tendency to rate low. You can remember from school how some teachers were dreaded because they were considered "low markers." The opposite is also true. You may have a tendency to mark everyone "up" because you are lenient, afraid to harm their future chances, or reluctant to discuss problems. Remember, being too lenient can cause problems later. People who think they are doing well will expect raises and promotions to match what you have told them about their performance.

Or you may be a victim of what statisticians call "central tendency." This is the temptation to think of everyone as average. The problem with these three tendencies is that they prevent us from being accurate in our assessments. That makes the appraisal not only unfair but less useful. One of the characteristics of highly successful managers is that they are able to differentiate among high, average, and low performers. If you tend to rate everyone in one category, you need to pay closer attention to what the employee has or has not achieved and begin to make better distinctions.

Another problem with trying to assess performance objectively is the tendency people have to claim credit for things that go right and to blame others or outside influences when things go wrong. If the work has not gone well, you may be inclined to blame the employee, but your employee will find other reasons, outside his or her own efforts, for the failure. And you may both be right. It may be a combination of both the employee's work performance and the external factors. You need to be careful that you don't wind up blaming one another for poor performance. Try to sort out the problems so you know what their causes really are.

Another issue, which seems to be part of human nature, is the tendency of managers to blame poor performance on weaknesses in the employee's character rather than on specific behavior or elements in the employee's environment (or heaven forbid the manager's own ineptitude). If Vic Shemsky isn't getting his sales reports in on time, it is because he's lazy or chronically late, or sloppy. It isn't because he is making more sales calls than anyone else and doesn't have time to write them all up, or that he doesn't see the need to do all that writing, or that he feels uncomfortable writing reports. If you ask Vic why he isn't writing his reports, you can be sure he won't say "because I'm lazy." Does this mean there is no such thing as a lazy person. No. But it does mean that we have to be careful that we don't take the easy way out when assessing performance and attribute failures to personality problems. Besides, we have already said that there isn't much we can do to change people's personalities. If we look for another cause for the problem, we may be able to come up with a viable solution.

This problem of personality is particularly hard to avoid if you don't get along well with the employee. If you don't like Vic, you are more likely to blame his late reports on his personality. If you like him, you will find another reason, a way of forgiving him. Our biases about race, sex, age, and nationality show up in subtle ways here too. Some people rate minorities and women lower than others; some expect so little of them that anything they accomplish seems like a miracle and gets very high marks; others bend over backward to give them a break and rate them higher than they deserve. Can you clear your mind of some of these biases? Can you be aware of how your own biases affect your judgment and unbalance your conclusions?

One of the really sneaky pitfalls may occur when you are doing appraisals on two or more people at a time. If you have just looked at the performance of a real "superstar," the next person's performance may pale by comparison, and you may give the second person a lower rating than is warranted. Conversely, an average performer may get a higher than warranted rating if you have just been wrestling with the problems of the worst person in your group.

Some people look as if they're trying very hard. As they work we are aware of the enormous effort they are putting in. We have a tendency to admire this industry and rate "tryers" high. Others may accomplish as much or more, but they make it look easy. They tend to be rated lower because we don't see their efforts. For instance, June does an excellent job as a product manager, but she doesn't stay as late or look as haggard as her colleagues. She's accomplishing her objectives, but Harry, her boss, doesn't see her spending long hours at her desk. Harry would probably scrutinize June's work less and admire her accomplishments more if she made the job seem hard. When you appraise performance, are you looking at how much sweat went into the work or how much good came out of it?

The last, and hardest, task is to reduce the distortion your own personality creates. We all have a tendency to reject people who have traits that are the opposite of our own, regardless of whether those traits affect their work. Let me give you an example. Art is a slob. His desk and his office are unbelievably messy. His boss's desk rarely contains anything but a piece of paper or two and a telephone. He tells Art that a sloppy desk is a sign of a sloppy mind. (Art wonders what an empty desk signifies.) The question is can Art's boss objectively measure Art's contribution and ignore the mess in Art's office? Given his personality, the boss would probably have trouble with that.

When you evaluate performance you have to decide whether the job was done well or poorly, but if everything isn't just as it should have been and you are going to correct the situation for the future, you also have to figure out why the work was unsatisfactory. Don't be too quick to assume that your employee just didn't try hard enough. Reconsider the factors you used to plan the job. Was it reasonable to begin with? In retrospect, does the work still seem to have been realistic? Did some unforeseen change take place in the environment? In looking for causes, adopt a problem-solving, not a blaming, mode.

One way to separate the symptoms from the problems is to look at skills and abilities, rather than attitudes. Whether you tend to be too hard or too lenient, this approach will help you overcome some of your biases and give your employee a fairer appraisal. Once people know that their work will be judged by what they accomplish, most of them will be more highly motivated, and will work harder, and achieve more. When you evaluate the performance of your people, you must look not only at the outcome but at the methods. Did this person exceed the objectives by running roughshod all over the rest of the staff? Were the work goals accomplished at the expense of others accomplishing theirs? When you appraise the performance of a person, you must look at what the person did or did not do, but you must also put those accomplishments in context. Otherwise you can breed blind ambition. For you to be an effective manager, your whole group has to be effective, and everyone in it has to be able to deal effectively with the rest of the organization. If your people are ruining one another's chances of success or the chances of people in other departments, you need to help them redefine "success." Think of the loss of productivity when people stand around and discuss how difficult it is to work with Bill or Grace. Consistent high performance over the long run is what we want to foster in our people, not short-term success that mortgages the future.

Getting Other Opinions

Often you can improve the accuracy of your own judgments and avoid some of the pitfalls we've just described by getting opinions from others who know the work of your employees. Other people probably already give you informal feedback on how your people are doing. Customers complain about or compliment your sales representatives. Other managers or supervisors casually mention a good job or a problem. You may want to stick a note in the file when you hear these things so you'll remember them at appraisal time. Better yet, you may want to seek out a balanced picture of your employees' performance by asking others who have observed them to share those observations with you. This way you will have more information on which to base your own evaluation. By having more than one perspective, you can avoid errors in judgment that stem from too narrow a view.

By asking for the evaluation rather than just passively accepting what others choose to tell you, you will get a more balanced view. Since many people think of making comments only when they have something to complain about, many informal comments are skewed toward the negative. By going to meet with other managers and asking for a more formal appraisal, you are more likely to get a thoughtful response. And you not only will make your own evaluation more reliable but you also will foster good relations with the people whose comments you solicit. They will feel flattered that you care about their opinions and know that you regard them as important.

If the employee you are evaluating hasn't worked for you for very long and there are others in your organization who have supervised the person in the past, you may want to make your own evaluation and then check it with the employee's previous boss. Of course, you will have read the previous evaluation in the employee's personnel file, but don't stop there. You know how written information can sometimes be distorted. Check out your interpretations in a discussion to make sure you understand what you've read.

You will want to get other opinions whenever you don't have an opportunity to observe your employee firsthand, for instance, when appraising salespeople who work from a different location. You might also seek other opinions when you feel it is difficult for you to be objective in your assessment. Sometimes you are just too close to the work to be able to see what is really happening. This is true especially if you don't get along very well with your employee. Sometimes another person can help you separate personality issues from issues of skill and job effectiveness. How, for instance, will I ever be able to see whether my managerial style prevents my people from doing the job. If I have good friends in the organization who can be honest and who can see what's happening in my group, I may be able to get that information from them.

Of course, you don't want to just accept the evaluations of others. You have to "evaluate the evaluation." We have said that you can't simply read the previous written evaluations. They may not be written clearly, you may misinterpret what they mean, or the previous supervisor may not have written in total honesty. You know that sometimes managers write things that are different from what they really feel, because they want to justify a raise or because they misguidedly think it's kinder to say only nice things. When you check out someone's previous written appraisal or ask for an evaluation from someone who has another perspective on your employee's work, ask for the same kind of specifics we have said are necessary from your own appraisal. Find out how that person came to conclusions and ask for examples of what the employee did or did not do. You should never accept character or personality evaluations. These are not helpful since they don't appraise performance. When two managers sit together and discuss personality, they are not appraising, they're simply gossiping.

Whatever another person tells you about your employee, be sure to screen the information for whatever biases that evaluator may have. You want information that can either validate or change your own opinion, not a new set of biases. You need to filter what you hear through your knowledge of the other evaluator's perspective. Don't just accept the opinion of another manager who may have some ax to grind by making your subordinate look either bad or good.

You may find that your more self-confident and ambitious employees may ask other managers for feedback on their performance or about their prospects with the firm. For the most part you should regard this as positive, unless you feel it is a sign that your employees are not getting enough of the right kind of help from you. If you aren't coaching and counseling as you should, then solve the problem by becoming more aware of the person's needs and doing what you can. Some managers would try to solve the problem by forbidding the employee to seek such advice outside the unit. That approach would only make the problem worse.

If your colleagues come to you for an appraisal of their employees, give the same kind of specific, thoughtful evaluation you would want from them. Certainly, you will not share appraisal information on anyone unless you know why and how it will be used. Those who seek information about how you view the work of your own or other managers' people must first be willing to tell you why they are interested in knowing what you think.

Prepare Your Employee to Appraise the Work

Many managers fear asking employees to do a self-appraisal. They feel employees will build themselves up and that it will then be impossible to get them to think realistically. Managers also feel that employees will not respond. These fears are largely unfounded if employees are asked to evaluate the work, rather than to give themselves a rating—a 3 or an "outstanding." We come here to the same issue raised earlier with managers' evaluations. We cannot ask employees to evaluate their own characters or to provide some overall description of themselves. That would put them severely on the defensive. The question we need to ask is How did the work go? We want employees to comment on the goals and objectives, whether they were accomplished and how well. To the extent that we have written a specific, measurable plan, it should be obvious whether or not the work has been accomplished.

Then why bother with employee self-evaluation? Well, having actually worked the plan, the employee will have many ideas on what that experience was like and how it went. Where there are still some leftover gray areas (there will be more of these in some kinds of work than in others), you will need to hear the employee's opinion about whether what happened was more on the positive or negative side. You will have discussed problems already, but you will want to hear the employee's opinion of how things ended up.

To be fair, you have to give your employee warning, I'd say at least a week, before the appraisal meeting. When you set up the date for the meeting with your employee, ask the person to come to the meeting prepared to talk about accomplishments, problems, new objectives for the next planning cycle, and personal and professional growth. Say what you expect to do at the meeting and how you expect to conduct it. Suggest rereading the work plan and job description, reviewing whatever reports are available and so forth. In other words, ask your employee to prepare for the meeting by reviewing the same material you will be looking at. Some managers share their entire file with the employee, even the notes they write to themselves and drop in the file throughout the year. My friend Howard Denmark allows his employees free access to the file anytime. He says, "It's in my desk, and they can read it or put stuff in it any time they like."

When you prepare your employee to do self-appraisal, set the meeting up as a discussion not as a courtroom where judgments will be made. Don't say, "I'm going to evaluate your performance." Say rather, "We're going to talk about your performance, review how things have gone with this year's work plan, and start working on next year's plan." In a certain sense, you will not make a formal evaluation of the employee until after the meeting since you will not write your evaluation until then. This sequence will make the discussion easier and more useful. The employee will not feel it is a judgment, and you will have the benefit of the employee's point of view before you write up an appraisal or make any decisions.

This brings us to the issue of that form from the personnel department. If there is such a form, give a copy of it to the employee. Say, "After our meeting, I will be filling out a form like this one based on our discussion." Tell the employee what will be done with the form and how it will be used. Of course, your experienced employees will already have gone through this process and will know the drill. Even new employees should have found out about the system at the very beginning, but this is a good time to remind the person of the procedure. Some managers review the blank form with the employee before the meeting. Then at the meeting boss and subordinate fill it out together. But don't have the form all filled out before the meeting. That will make the discussion seem like a mere formality.

Always take care in this preappraisal setup to assure the employee that this will be a positive and helpful discussion. If you have an open and easy working relationship with the person, this will be easy. If the relationship has been cool, it may be difficult to establish the right openness and trust. If the appraisal discussion is going to be productive, you must start early and work out your thornier communications difficulties. Otherwise the appraisal discussion will have little value.

Planning the Discussion

Once you have gathered the information, made your own analysis, and set up the meeting with your employee, you will need to plan the discussion. Even though you are going to encourage the employee to participate fully in the discussion, you will want to know where you want the discussion to go so you can keep it on track. Full participation by the employee is a wonderful goal, but this does not mean that you give up control.

The first rule to follow here is to limit the objectives and the topics of the discussion. When you talk about sitting down to review six months or a year of a person's work life and to plan the next six months or a year, you must concentrate on what is important and not let the conversation stray into trivia. There is no time in a thorough appraisal and planning meeting for trivia. Besides, focusing on trivial matters may give the employee the impression that you are a nitpicker or that you feel minutiae are critical. Instead, look over the list of things you might discuss and pick those that will make a real difference.

If you are looking at areas of improvement for your employee, you will want to limit the number of things you want the person to try to improve. No one can take a long laundry list of their supposed faults and start correcting them all. We all need to try to improve a little at a time. Most people can't even listen to a long list of their supposed faults. And as you plan this part of the discussion, you may want to have a few suggestions ready about how your employee can overcome the difficulties. But don't make official decisions about the method. Decide that at the meeting and pretty much leave the steps involved up to the employee. It's critical that you get the employee's commitment to these performance improvement goals and that will be easier if the person can say how the goal will be accomplished.

The culmination of your planning will be to make a specific agenda for the meeting. There is a general agenda at the end of this chapter to guide you.

Anticipating Problems

You may say anticipating problems is what you always do when you think of performance appraisal. The problem is that many of us anticipate problems in a vague or unrealistic way. We expect things to happen that are very unlikely; we never really put a face on the monster we fear. This leads to a general dislike for performance appraisal and then to a reluctance to do it. I suggest we get very concrete and have a plan ready for handling the real problems that might occur during the meeting.

The most common problem is that managers worry that the employee will reject the manager's evaluation and take a belligerent attitude. I don't know how often this occurs, but I'm certain that you can minimize the risk of it occurring if the employee understands that the appraisal will be based not on personality but on accomplishments and expectations that were clearly communicated at the outset.

Employees will respond more positively if they are treated with respect. This means that their ideas, feelings, and concerns are taken into consideration by their managers. You can say some pretty negative things to people, but if you say them with respect they will have the hoped-for effect. The next chapter details the techniques of supportive communication techniques that will help you communicate emotionally charged subjects.

If you anticipate negative reactions for all your appraisals, you may just be insecure about your ability to do the job well. There is only one cure for that. Learn what you can. Take the techniques from this and other books and try them out. Use the ones that work for you until you begin to be more comfortable with the skill. If you are going to continue to pursue a career in management, there is no way to avoid performance appraisal. You might as well master it.

Perhaps it is only certain appraisals that make you anxious. Examine which ones. Are they only the negative ones? If so, you may need to work on your communications skills so that you feel better about your ability to get criticism across gracefully. And remember, most people do not look gleefully upon the idea of criticizing another person. Those who do probably have some serious problems of their own.

Do appraisals of certain employees give you pause? Why? What are their similarities? Are they all older than you? Are they all members of the opposite sex? Or do you have trouble simply because you don't get along so well with certain members of your staff? Whatever the cause, you will be better able to cope with, and perhaps solve, the problem if you understand it.

If you ordinarily don't feel so negative, but a particular appraisal bothers you, it may be that you need to think over your conclusions. If you are reluctant to discuss them because you are unsure of them, perhaps you need to gather more information or reanalyze the issues. Certainly if you haven't faith in your own judgments, your employee will have even more trouble accepting what you say. No matter how hard you try to put on a confident face, consciously or subconsciously your employee will know you are unsure and reject your conclusions. Perhaps this is the basis of much of the difficulty that many of us have with performance appraisal. Deep down we know how hard it is to make a fair judgment of someone's work, and not feeling secure, we telegraph our underlying insecurity to the employee who either doubts our word or, more likely, adds our insecurity to his or her own. If all of this is so, the only solution I can think of is to develop our skills for analyzing how well the job was done. Then the careful, explicit planning and the unambiguous communication of our expectations up front become doubly important.

Accentuate the Positive

Most books and training programs on performance appraisal concentrate heavily on how to handle problems and how to make negative feedback palatable. This subject will get a good deal of attention in the next two chapters. It is true that many managers have a great deal of trouble with negatives and criticisms. But it is just as difficult for some people to give compliments. And this is a critical skill for managers. In fact, a case could be made that complimenting good performance is so important that if we had to choose between giving only compliments or only criticism, we should choose to give only compliments.

First of all, compliments give people what psychologists call "positive reinforcement" for their behavior. When someone does something and is rewarded by praise for that action, that person is likely to do the same thing again. Behavior can be shaped by people's need for praise and attention. Managers can use this powerful tool to guide the work of their people.

And praise for good work adds to people's self-confidence. You are aware, I am sure, of the link between self-confidence and high performance. In fact, more people fail or are stymied in their careers by a lack of confidence than by any other single factor. By learning to praise our people, we can enhance their self-images and let them know that we hold them in high regard. This feeling of self-worth will draw out their inner motivations. Because they feel we appreciate their efforts, they will be willing to give more.

If you are a manager who feels uncomfortable giving praise, you may not give it as freely as you should. This might mean that most of what your people hear from you is negative, and you could be giving them the impression that the efforts they make mean nothing to you. If your criticisms outweigh your compliments, they will be unwilling to give the extra bit since it will only seem to go unnoticed.

Praise is a reward for good performance and people see it that way, just as they see raises and promotions as rewards. It is certainly the least costly reward you can give. It is a way you can encourage your under-achievers and reward your best people. Speaking of your best people these are the ones you can easily forget. As we have said, your not-so-good performers will need lots of attention, and in the rush to get everything done it is easy to forget to give your best people the praise they deserve.

If compliments are so wonderful, since they make people feel so good and they are so useful, why is it that people find them so difficult to give? Well even though praise can have all the good effects we have seen, just like anything else, people have to learn how to handle it. This is true of both givers and receivers.

If you are a person who finds praise hard to take, you may find it very difficult to give. People who lack confidence in themselves often find compliments difficult to accept. They become embarrassed when they receive them, and therefore see the act of giving them as embarrassing too. Men are more often likely to find it embarrassing to give compliments, especially to other men.

Some managers worry about giving praise because they fear giving people what when I was a kid was called "a big head." In those days parents worried about this a lot. If your kid got good marks on her report card you said "keep trying" because you were afraid that if you said "great job" that would be the end of the effort. We believe today that the opposite is true: Praise can make people try harder if it is given skillfully and accepted readily.

What makes praise hard for some people to take? As I said before, it embarrasses them, and it does this because most of us have been brought up to believe that bragging is wrong. We extend this taboo against bragging and begin to feel that graciously accepting a compliment is the same as tooting your own horn. Have you ever complimented someone on a new piece of clothing only to get an immediate rundown on how she bought it on sale or an explanation that his wife really picked it out or it's really old. We tend to feel that to be polite we must somehow deny the praise we receive.

Some people are automatically suspicious of those who praise them. They expect all praise to be flattery and assume that anyone who praises them must have some ulterior motive. Other people see compliments and praise as just one of the social graces. A person who says something nice is just giving a compliment to be polite. How many times have you heard the phrase, "Oh, you're just saying that"?

For all of these reasons, people often hear praise and outwardly accept it graciously, but feel more hurt or embarrassed than pleased. If they do this, all the potential positive effects of the praise are lost. We can, however, learn to give praise so that it will have all the positive effects we want it to have.

First there are a bunch of things to avoid. Number one is the main bugaboo of this book so far: vagueness. Avoid general, indefinite statements, whether positive or negative.

If you are being positive, be positive. Don't give a person a compliment and then follow it with a complaint. People will wind up waiting for the "but." This is important not only if you are conducting an appraisal, but particularly if you are speaking in front of a third party.

As with all performance feedback, don't talk about the person's personality or character. Praising a person's character is not as harmful as criticizing it, but this is still not a good idea. If you feel you have the right to judge whether people are good, you may feel you also have the right to judge whether they are bad. It's best to avoid expressing this kind of judgment.

Some people who want to give a genuine compliment and find themselves too embarrassed to do it will make an insult out of the compliment. For example, someone might say, "That's a great tie, Jack. Your wife must be picking out your clothes these days." This does no good; Jack winds up feeling bad about himself and the giver of the "compliment."

Equally harmful is the compliment that always involves someone else. No one wants self-worth always to depend on being better than someone else. One wonders why another person is always the yardstick by which one is measured. This fosters a sort of false "sibling rivalry" between employees. If you are going to compliment someone it should be on the person's own merits. This is another way that a good performance plan helps. If you compliment a person's work, you can do it in relation to the plan, and you don't need to have any other basis of comparison.

Use Compliments Constructively

Some managers will use thinly disguised compliments as criticism. They are uncomfortable with giving performance feedback or they value their own wit more than they value their subordinates' good performance. These people can make a genuine compliment impossible to accept because they have "polluted" so many of their own compliments. People get so used to getting insults thinly veiled as compliments that they suspect all compliments. Under this heading come such barbs as:

Damning with faint praise. The eighteenth-century English poet Alexander Pope used this phrase to described what critics in the papers often do: give a paltry compliment where a bigger one is expected. In business, this comes out in statements like, "Well, gee, Margaret, I guess I should be grateful. After all, you did get some words on paper and you spelled them all correctly." If we sometimes express hostility in the form of faint praise, people won't trust our sincerity.

The "gotcha" compliment. This one starts out as a compliment, but ends up as criticism. Bosses who are afraid to make people over-confident will use this technique, for example, "Well, Hank, you did a great job getting the data together and analyzing the results. Remember though, that when you report this to the executive committee, you have to do a decent job. No more fidgeting and mumbling." This sort of comment leaves someone who has just done a good job fearing failure in the future. The person doesn't get a chance to enjoy present success. And if there is no enjoyment, there is less motivation to try hard in the future.

The "patronizing parent" compliment. Here the manager really wants to encourage the employee to do better, but the "compliment" comes out like this, "I know you are a bright woman, Alice. If you would only learn to listen to the clients more carefully, I'm sure you will be able to sell Allied on our proposal."

Enough of those remarks and the employee will start to wince as soon as she hears the compliment.

There are probably other forms of this type of "praise," but you get the message. If you engage in this kind of "compliment," you will forfeit your ability to use the sincere compliment, which can be one of your most powerful tools as a manager. Instead, here is how to handle praise effectively:

Be specific. Always tell the people you are praising exactly what they did that you found praiseworthy. This will increase the chances that they will learn from your compliment what the job requires.

Be direct. Say as simply and clearly as you can that you admire thus-and-so that the person has done. Even if it is difficult for you, learn to bite the bullet, look your employee in the eye and say, "Solving that problem took a lot of extra time, Jo. I appreciate your staying late and getting it done."

Directness also means that you talk to the person, not send your message through someone else. If the person does not work directly for you, but for someone who reports to you, talk to both of them. A compliment that comes from the boss's boss can be particularly powerful. And note that I said talk to the person. Sending a thank-you gift is a great idea, but only if you have expressed yourself by talking to the person as well.

Do it often. If your praise comes very infrequently, people may be suspicious of it just because it is so unusual. They will ask themselves if you are saying something nice because you want something.

Say it first. The novelist Kurt Vonnegut says he hates the words "I love you" because the only possible answer is, "I love you, too." Don't make your people think that you give praise only as a response to flattery.

One way to enhance the power of your praise is to take opportunities to give it publicly. Criticism must be given in private. But praise can be given in public if a natural opportunity presents itself. This both enhances its value to the receiver and sends a message to others about what kind of performance you admire.

If you have employees who have trouble accepting praise, teach them how to accept it. Years ago my friend and colleague Earl Garris taught me to accept praise gracefully. I had a lot of trouble receiving compliments then, and Earl noticed this. His method of teaching me to accept them may be useful to you. He first pointed out the problem—every time he complimented me, I found some reason other than my own efforts to credit for my success. He insisted that each time he praised me that I say nothing but "thank you" and count to ten. If I started my old routine, he reminded me that it was polite to say "thank you." It took a while, but not too long, and he helped a great deal. I learned more than just how to accept compliments graciously. I learned to enjoy my own successes more fully. You can help the people who work for you do this. They'll never forget it.

What about Criticism

With all this talk about praise, you may think that I feel there is no room for criticism in performance appraisal. That's not entirely correct. There are times when we will have negative things to say about what our employees have done, and we need to talk about how to handle that. We will deal with the subject at length when we discuss poor performers in a later chapter, but let's talk a little about it now.

First, the important thing to remember about criticism is that pure criticism doesn't usually motivate people to improve. It makes them feel bad about themselves and may make them so defensive that they spend more time telling themselves that they're not so bad and not enough time thinking about whether the criticism is valid and how to correct the problem. Appraisals are more likely to get positive results if they emphasize the positive. Some managers, however, tend to emphasize the negative. Like judges watching Olympic skaters, they look for reasons to take points off. Their appraisals tend to emphasize people's mistakes and failures. Because this approach is so prevalent, I push people very hard to make the appraisal a session about the employee's strengths and successes as well as a review of the person's weaknesses and failures. Building up people's confidence is a big part of getting them to succeed. Hence my emphasis on praise. But I admit that criticism is sometimes unavoidable.

Everybody talks about criticism as being "constructive," but some of us have no idea what makes criticism constructive rather than destructive. The difference is really quite simple. Destructive criticism merely states what the failure has been, but offers no way of changing the situation and no encouragement to employees that they can do better. To make your criticism constructive:

1. **Be specific.** Here's our old friend again. State what you feel needs to be changed in behavioral terms. Say what the person did or didn't do and give one or two representative examples. Never dwell on the person's failures. Brevity is important here. And note that I said failures not failings. Never speak about problems as being part of the person's character.

2. **Offer suggestions about what to do instead.** "Here's what you have been doing; here's what might work better." That's the approach to take. Often you can state the problem and work with the employee to work out alternative courses of action.

3. **Encourage the employee.** An expression of your faith that the person can make the necessary change will go a long way to making it seem possible and bringing out the employee's motivation to try.

4. **Give your support.** Find out from your employee how you can be helpful. If you are willing to make the effort, then maybe the employee will too.

Some managers, in an effort to be kind, will avoid saying anything negative to the employee. This is pure cowardice. Your job is to control the work, and you don't do it by fibbing to a person about performance. Some managers have been known to go so far as to write the problems down for the file, then soft-pedal them to the employee. Fairness dictates that what you write and what you say be the same.

What about Personal Problems

When you analyze your employee's performance, you may come to the conclusion that the lack of results is caused by some special problem the employee has: difficulties at home, financial worries, a drinking, drug, or psychological problem. These are difficult things for a manager to handle. By criticizing performance, you can make the person's problem worse.

Watch for deteriorating performance. You may suspect personal problems as the cause if the employee had been doing a good job but lately has been falling behind. Some experts estimate that as many as 10 percent of U.S. workers have personal problems that affect their work performance. These can also cause other problems: lower morale among fellow employees, high absenteeism, accidents on the job. In the past, employees with problems were just fired. Today, employers realize that an employee represents an investment and an asset. It is better to try to rescue the person and restore good performance than to start over training a new person. Besides, you may face legal problems if you terminate a person with medical or financial difficulties. You can help rehabilitate a troubled employee. First of all, never treat this sort of thing casually. You must take anything you do very seriously. You need to decide whether this is something you are going to approach with the employee. You may want to skip the discussion altogether and get the professionals from the medical or personnel department to handle the entire problem. You may want to go to them for advice about what you can or cannot do.

If you decide to meet with the employee yourself, never treat the problem as if it is the employee's fault. Using a matter-of-fact tone, tell the person what you have observed and why it is a problem on the job. You may be so nervous about bringing the subject up that you will talk too much. Say little and whatever you say, say it quietly. Take the pressure off the employee by saying that you feel that this is not something the person did on purpose.

Keep away from amateur psychoanalysis. Why the problem exists— why Lucy drinks or Marvin always feels persecuted—is not your business. It would be tactless, and could exacerbate the problem, for you to indulge in this sort of speculation. Offer to help the person in any way you can. But don't try to replace the professionals. Financial, psychological, or family problems can be complex and difficult. Beware of taking simplistic steps to correct them. When in doubt, get advice from an expert in the field.

Assessing employees' performance and helping them improve and grow requires all the sensitivity we as bosses can muster. This is true especially when we must deal with the troubled employee.

Summary

- Schedule the performance appraisal meeting.

  When

  - You and your employee can give full attention to the subject.
  - You will have time to do it justice.

  Where

  - You will have total privacy.
  - You can sit and face each other.
  - On "neutral territory" if that will make a difference.

- Once you set the date, keep it.
- To assess your employee's performance, review:
  - Work plan for the period
  - Job description
  - Notes in the employee's file
  - Reports of production, sales, and so forth
- Ask your employee to do the same.
- In appraising performance, beware of:
  - Harshness
  - Excessive leniency
  - Central tendency
  - Blaming the person's "personality"
  - Overlooking problems outside the employee's control
  - Biases that relate to race, sex, age, or nationality
  - Letting the last appraisal you did influence your thinking on this one
  - Giving high ratings only to those who "look" as if they're working
- Look for reasons why objectives were not met.
- Get opinions from others if:
  - Their observations will make your own assessment more accurate.
  - The person hasn't worked for you for very long.
  - Others have more frequent contact with your employee.
  - When your relationship with the employee threatens your objectivity.
  - When you feel your management style may be a key factor in the employee's performance.
- Ask for specifics, not just general comments, about your employee's work.
- Weigh the opinions of other managers in the light of their perspective on the employee and the job.

- Prepare your employee to do a self-appraisal by:
  - Stating the purpose of the appraisal meeting
  - Presenting the meeting as a mutually beneficial discussion, not a judging session
  - Giving the employee all the information you have for making your assessment
  - Setting up the appointment at least a week in advance to give the employee time to prepare
- If your company has an appraisal form, fill it out after, not before, the meeting.
- To keep the appraisal meeting under control:
  - Set objectives for it.
  - Limit the objectives to what is most important in the employee's performance.
- Anticipate problems that may occur during the meeting. Know ahead of time how you plan to respond.
- Praise is one of your most powerful management tools. To use it effectively:
  - Be specific.
  - Be direct.
  - Do it often.
  - Say it first.
- To make criticism constructive:
  - Make it specific.
  - Offer suggestions about what to do.
  - Offer encouragement by expressing your faith that the person can change.
  - Offer your own help.
- If personal problems—financial or marital difficulties, drinking, drugs, and so on—are the causes of poor performance, seek advice about what to do from professionals.

Agenda for Performance Appraisal Meeting

- Manager opens the meeting:
  - States objectives of the session
  - Sets tone of openness and free discussion
- Employee presents self-assessment.
- Manager responds to the employee's remarks.
- Both look for causes of any problems.
- Both set objectives and work out a plan for the next period.

Chapter **6**

Conducting the Appraisal Interview

If you are playing basketball with someone and you want to pass him the ball, you will throw it in a certain way. You will throw the ball hard and directly to the person if you intend it to be caught. If you don't throw it hard enough, it will never reach its destination. If you throw the ball at the other player's head, he will deflect rather than catch it. Giving feedback on performance is like passing a basketball. It must be given directly and clearly, but in such a way as to be accepted—"caught"—by the employee.

The performance appraisal meeting is the forum for this feedback, and it has three objectives:

1. To learn what your employees think of their own performance and what their primary motivations are.
2. To give your own assessment of what employees have accomplished. To praise good performance so it will continue and to call attention to needs for improvement.
3. To plan for future good performance.

The appraisal interview is a real bugaboo for managers and supervisors. This is where things most often go wrong. Even if you have done everything right before the meeting, you can still ruin all your good work if the meeting itself doesn't go well. Fortunately, there are some easy-to-learn techniques to help you conduct a meeting that is productive and comfortable both for you and your employee. First let's look at an overview of how the meeting will go:

- You will state the objectives and set the tone for the meeting.
- Your employee will give a self-appraisal.
- You will add your comments.
- Together you will discuss and plan for future work.

Begin the meeting by stating the objectives and sharing your agenda with the employee. Then take some time to set a tone of cooperation and to help the employee relax. Remember that regardless of the person's performance your employee is likely to feel tense. Fear of criticism and embarrassment, anticipation of what effects this session will have on career, next raise, or status in the organization will make the prospect of performance appraisal anxiety producing. I find it useful to be direct and talk about nervousness, acknowledge that it is natural, and reassure the person about the purpose of the meeting. Use a quiet, forthright tone of voice. By dealing with your employee's anxiety, you will also help to control your own.

Then ask your employee for an appraisal of the work. Remember, both you and the employee will talk about the work and how it went. Neither of you is going to be addressing overall ratings or character traits.

Often supervisors and managers object strongly to my advice to let employees speak first. They fear it will mean that employees will say a whole lot of great things about themselves and that it will be the supervisor's job to argue them out of that lofty position.

Actually for most people nothing could be further from the truth. Most people, say 80 percent, will not brag or boast. They will try to give a balanced view of their performance and will probably even play down the pluses and play up the minuses. Some will be reluctant to talk at all. A few will talk only about the positives or express a better opinion of their own performance than you have. Sometimes these will be people who really believe they are doing better than they are, probably because they did not understand what was required or what was most important. Sometimes those who anticipate a low rating will try to "tough it out" by giving a glowing account of themselves. There are easy techniques for dealing with each situation.

Let the Employee Speak First

By having the employee speak first, you make things easier for both of you. It makes more sense for a number of reasons.

You Learn More

If you, the manager, give your opinion first, your employee will be reluctant to speak. The person will not want to contradict your negative judgments or to agree with your positive ones. You will thus learn very little about what your employee is thinking. Knowing how your employee thinks about job performance can give you the information you need to proceed with the performance improvement or goal setting discussion. It will help you take the right tack with the person. It will also help you learn how confident the employee is, and this information will help you take the right approach to any negative observations you may want to make.

There will be instances when you will get what the employee thinks you want to hear rather than what the person really believes. You may need to draw the person out to get behind the first response. Or you may need to just be aware of this dynamic.

You Avoid a Certain Amount of Defensiveness

If the manager speaks first, the employee may automatically respond defensively. Besides, once the manager has spoken, what can the employee say? Your employee may feign agreement with what you have said even if she believes your assessment is wrong. This may lead to resentment or hostility, but never to real performance improvement, which is what you're after. Even if you are speaking with an employee whose performance is outstanding, you will want to hear the person's own story, and you are unlikely to get it if you speak first.

Your Meeting Will Be More Productive

Studies have shown that performance appraisal is more effective and employees are more satisfied with it if managers emphasize mutual problem solving and encourage employee participation.

This approach will also allow you to act more like a counselor than a judge. If you seem like an advisor rather than an authoritarian, your employees will be less tense and more able to be open to what you have to say.

And you may feel tense and anxious yourself. Often the anxiety managers feel about performance appraisal meetings stems from their discomfort with the role of judge. If judging makes you anxious, don't do it. Being a counselor or advisor is much more comfortable as well as infinitely more productive.

Listen carefully while your employee is speaking. Listening, you probably have heard, is one of mankind's most neglected skills. Instead of listening, managers are most likely to begin thinking about whether or not they agree with what employees are saying. The employee says, for example, "I think I've improved in getting my reports in on time." And the manager immediately begins to think, "Oh yeah? What about the sales summary for the first quarter? That was three days late, and Ferguson was on my back the whole time, and I have to have him on my side if I'm going to sell my new marketing strategy . . ." And on and on. In an appraisal interview, it is easy for both parties to engage in what has been called defensive self-listening. Put your own thoughts aside for a while and really listen to what your employee is saying. As I have said, this is important input for your own plan of action.

Listen actively. Here are some suggestions on how to improve your listening skills. (You may feel the need to take a course or seek out some more thorough way of developing these important skills.)

- Listen for emotional as well as for logical content. Watch the employee's facial expressions and body movements for clues to the hidden meaning of what the person is saying.
- Summarize in your mind the major points of what the person has said. Feed back this summary to the speaker from time to time.
- If you are unsure of what the person is saying, gently interrupt to make sure.
- Say what you think the speaker is feeling.

These active responses to what the employee is saying (rather than the passive way many people listen) will show the employee that you are interested and are paying full attention.

Suppose your employee says very little. Don't be too quick to give up on getting your employee's opinion. Self-appraisal is hard. If you have followed the advice in the previous chapter and given your employee clear instructions about what you expect, the person should be prepared. If your invitation to speak first doesn't elicit an immediate response, draw the employee out by asking open-ended questions. (Open-ended questions require more than a yes or no answer.) For instance:

Closed question: Do you feel the new process installation was a success?

Open question: How do you feel about the latest new process installation?

Since you will have copies of the performance plan handy, you may want to suggest that the employee use the plan as a jumping-off point. If your employee seems reluctant to talk, it may help if you feed in a few of your own ideas to "prime the pump." By all means, don't take the employee's reticence as encouragement to dominate the conversation. If you begin to express your own opinions strongly, you may cut off any possibility of a response. It's also good to begin by asking questions about some positive aspect of performance. If all else fails, you may have to say, "I feel you're a little reluctant to talk. Can you tell me why?"

I suppose it's possible that nothing you say or do will get the employee to talk. Or you may have just the opposite problem. You may have an employee who talks on and on. The active listening responses we've already covered will help you control this sort of problem. If the flood of words concerns problems the employee has, just listening can help. Employees need to let off steam. If the work period has been particularly frustrating, your employee may need an outlet for pent-up emotions. Once the employee ventilates these feelings, you can get down to the business of solving the problems. If you try to stop the emotions from surfacing, you may find they will hamper the employee's ability to approach the problems logically.

Some employees who have not achieved their goals may want to "pass the buck"—blame other people for their lack of progress. You have to get these employees to accept responsibility, and you won't do this by arguing. Ask questions to direct their thinking, and if you can get them to accept responsibility for even a small part of the problem, be supportive. A person who has admitted even a small failure needs sympathy and encouragement. For example, you can say, "John, I know how hard it is to admit that you could have done better. But I'm glad you can see so clearly what happened. That's the first step to correcting the problem, and I know you want to correct it and that you can." Words like this will help the person accept even broader responsibility.

Once you have heard the person out, you should respond. But don't start right in with your appraisal. Begin by responding to what the person has said. (Besides enhancing the process, this forces you to listen. You can't respond to words you haven't heard.) First say what in the employee's self-appraisal you agree with. In this way, you can make a relatively negative comment seem rather positive and easy to take. For instance:

> ***Employee:*** One area where I really want to improve is in work-ing more with the team. I feel I get my own work done well, but the things that involve others are hard for me.

> ***You:*** You've done a good job of self-analysis. I agree that team work is something you need to work on.

How much easier it is to hear what might be a negative comment couched in such terms. Remember that your objective in having this discussion is to come to agreements with your employee. The more agreements you can make, the better. This is another advantage of having your employee speak first.

Be sure to give positive as well as negative feedback. Remember from the previous chapter that validation is just as important as constructive criticism.

Next, you will say what you disagree with. Sometimes you will be disagreeing with a negative judgment your employee has made about her own performance.

> ***Employee:*** I think my reject rate is too high.

> ***You:*** Margaret, you said that your reject rate is too high. That was a concern last time we talked, but I think you've made signifi-cant improvements in that. For the past two months your rate has been below the department's average. I call that good progress.

You see, many people will test to see if you've noticed their improve-ment by saying that a previous problem is still a problem. You get to show you have noticed *(and you'd better notice)*.

Last, you will present your own appraisal. Provided your perfor-mance plan was well made, it should be fairly easy for you to go over the expectations that your employee hasn't covered in the self-appraisal and state how the person met them. You may find that your employee has covered the same things you want to talk about, but has just looked at them from a different point of view. Often employees will put the emphasis on the how—how well they got along with others or how they invented a short cut to get a job done. Managers will be more likely to emphasize the what—what was done on time, what was late, or what the employee knows and doesn't know. These differences are a natural outgrowth of your differing perspectives on the job. You may have to help your employee see the work from a new perspective.

In presenting your viewpoint, two things are important: what you say and how you say it. First let's deal with what you say. Remember, as we discussed in the chapter on preparing for the meeting, that you are not going to cover everything in depth. People just cannot deal with too many things at once. If someone needs lots of improvement, you will want to have limited objectives. Cover each point of the performance plan, but concentrate on those items that will become major inputs to the new plan. Again, that is not to say that you will ignore the positives or touch on them only lightly. This is your chance to make sure that the positive behavior continues. Speak of the positives specifically, and make sure that your employee knows how much you appreciate them. And make sure that you don't wind up with a long list of trivial little problems. That kind of picky perfectionism can sour a good performer.

Now let's deal with how you say it. This is a big subject. The old adage "It's not what you say, it's how you say it" applies to nothing if not performance appraisal. You can tell a person she is the most outstanding performer in the department and make her feel suspicious or you can tell a person that he has bad breath and make him feel you have done him a big favor. It's all in how you say it. The big problem here is to avoid making people feel defensive. To do that you need to understand what causes defensive behavior and how to avoid it.

Most defensive behavior stems from a feeling of being attacked. The attack can be real or imagined; the response will be the same. In the appraisal interview there are many opportunities to put the other person on the defensive. We can do this by making statements that seem harsh or by making the person feel that we are making judgments about character rather than performance on the job. When we talked about the importance of performance planning, we talked about the difficulties involved in a system that was based on the supervisor's opinion of the subordinate. You will recall that the major difficulty lay in our assessing what kind of a person the employee is instead of assessing what the employee did or didn't do. So the first thing to remember in learning to avoid conflict during the meeting is to concentrate on what the person has or has not done and not on what kind of person the employee is. Even if the company has a form that requires you to make judgments about things like "cooperativeness," you are not going to speak about character traits. In a later chapter there is information on how to deal with the existence of such a form. If you have to fill one out, read the advice given there, but don't let that form become the basis of your comments. That could create unnecessary defensiveness.

Present Criticism Supportively

Avoid presenting your opinions in a way that seems:

Evaluative

How, you might ask, can you evaluate performance without being evaluative? Well, of course, you can't. The trick here is to describe the person's performance or accomplishments and not pass critical judgment on the person as a person. One way to do this is to express your thoughts in terms of what you think or feel or observe. For example: Instead of saying, "*You* are uncooperative," say, "*I* notice that when Maria is overloaded, you seem reluctant to pitch in and help her out. Is there a reason for that?"

Controlling

Don't try to force the person to your point of view. If you differ in your judgments, treat the difference as a problem to be solved. Look for collaborative ways to get to the bottom of the problem and come up with a mutually agreeable solution. Remember that agreement given grudgingly is unlikely to lead to enthusiastic behavior change on the employee's part.

Strategic

There's a great temptation to manipulate the other person into agreeing through games and tricks. A favorite way to do this is to ask a question that isn't really a question. For instance, the boss asks, "What do you suppose happened when that report was three days late?" The boss already knows the answer to the question and is just trying to shame the employee into submission. Questions like this lead the person to a point where the boss can say "gotcha." Here's an example of a series of "gotchas":

> *Manager:* What do you suppose happened when that report was three days late?
>
> *Employee:* I don't know.

Manager: Ferguson was on my back for three days, that's what happened. And how do you suppose that makes me look?

Employee: Pretty bad, I guess.

Manager: And that's just how you look to me.

Instead, we need to be straightforward and honest in expressing what we feel. It would be better to say, "Because your report was late, mine was late too. That made me angry because I don't want to be seen as a person who misses deadlines."

Superior

Managers and supervisors who lack confidence in themselves often feel the need to assert their authority by trying to show who is boss or by putting other people down. This is always a bad idea and never so much as in a performance appraisal meeting. It is clear to your subordinate that you are the boss. There is no need to assert it by pulling superiority moves at this meeting. You don't need to call attention to the fact that you are the boss, or refer to your higher level of education, or greater length of service. If instead you enter the discussion with mutual respect and trust, you will have a comfortable and productive meeting.

Neutral

Many managers and supervisors feel that being objective is a most important aspect of performance appraisal. In a certain sense this is correct. But sometimes this search for objectivity leads the manager to act neutral and detached during the meeting. This attitude will make employees feel as if they are being treated as objects rather than as people. Your appraisal will be objective if it is based on what a person has or has not done and if it avoids judging a person's character. But you must be empathetic. Identify with the feelings and problems of your employee. You could say, "The customer is always right." On the other hand, you can show that you sympathize with your employee's position by saying, "I know how hard it is to keep your cool when a customer's request seems unreasonable. The customer is not always right, but we have to treat him as if he is."

Certain

It is easy for managers and supervisors to make the mistake of coming across as dogmatic and close-minded. If your mind seems closed on a subject, the best you can hope for is grudging agreement. Start your discussion in a provisional frame of mind. Be willing to experiment with the ideas, values, and attitudes of the other person. From this starting point you may be able to come to an agreement. Instead of putting yourself in a win-lose position, you look for the win-win—the course of action that gets the job done but allows everyone to keep his or her dignity.

You can see then that your position as a manager is to be supportive of your employee. You show your support by being:

Descriptive

Problem-oriented

Spontaneous

Equal

Empathetic

Provisional

Here are some other ways to reduce the employee's defensiveness:

- Schedule the meeting when the employee is feeling positive.
- Keep channels of communication open all during the year. If you or your employee have been harboring hostilities, you will both enter the performance appraisal discussion feeling defensive.

If you get into a win-lose discussion, you will have no way of rescuing the conversation. You will feel you have to win the argument, and since you are the boss, you will win. But it's unlikely that you will win your employee's enthusiastic cooperation.

Many managers have had training in or read about Transactional Analysis. If you have, you will find it easy to analyze the performance appraisal interview from the standpoint of the Parent-Adult-Child model. The temptation in the performance appraisal interview is for the supervisor or manager to take the role of the Parent. This tactic almost forces the employee to take the role of the Child and is uncomfortable for both parties. The supervisor feels threatened because he or she knows that the power a parent has over a child is really not part of a supervisor's relationship with a subordinate. The supervisor may then become hardened in a position while trying to "tough out" the situation and make the employee submit. All this, of course, tends to make the employee take a defensive Child stance. This stance may lead to temper tantrums of the "who are you to tell me what to do" variety. Or it may lead to the "woe is me" pouting or crying position. Having an employee start to cry (especially when the employee is a woman and the manager a man) is a fear frequently expressed in performance appraisal training programs. The way to avoid this is to do the performance appraisal from the Adult mode; that is, speak about facts, be reasonable and rational in your statements, and treat the person as an equal who has an equal stake in what is happening. This allows your employee to respond in the Adult mode as well and keeps the meeting on an even keel.

The principles many people have learned in assertiveness training programs are also useful in understanding the dynamics of the performance appraisal interview. Assertive behavior on the part of supervisors or managers is the most appropriate. That is, managers must state their thoughts clearly, in a straightforward manner, and with confidence. Aggressive behavior on the part of managers is inappropriate. This aggression may take the form of threats about a worker's future employment or other possible retaliation for bad performance, or it may be just a negative opinion stated with too much force. In response, employees may also become aggressive and act with outright hostility or, depending on their personalities, may become passive and try to seem very accepting. Many employees disagree with what their bosses say but are afraid to say so. This acquiescent behavior, however, will merely mask underlying hostility and the discussion will probably not lead to a willing, much less enthusiastic, behavior change.

Whatever the results of your assessment, your best bet for making the appraisal meeting a positive, productive experience for both of you is to turn any negatives into positive action plans. You will always end your appraisal meeting by picking up the planning cycle. In other words, the cycle will look like this:

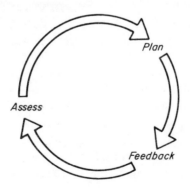

If you have found significant need for improvement, you may need to spend some time clarifying your basic expectations with your employee. This may lead to some changes or reclarification of the position description or list of basic job responsibilities. Once your employee understands the problems with the performance, ask for a plan of action for correcting the mistakes. The employee should formulate this plan with your guidance.

If your employee has performed very well, you will want to validate the good performance by compliments. Then you will set new objectives that will stretch the person's capacity and provide a real challenge. A need for improvement in the present job may lead you to set some personal improvement objectives. Good performance may indicate that the person has potential to move up in the organization. If so, you may want to set some personal growth objectives to help the person prepare for the next step needed. Whatever the situation, the meeting will end on a positive note because you will both have your plans for the future in hand when you part company.

At the end of the meeting, summarize all that has transpired. Two written documents should come out of the meeting: your written evaluation of the employee's performance and a write-up of the work plan. We have talked about the work plan in Chapter 3. Let's talk about the performance evaluation here.

First of all, you need to document your appraisal meeting. You don't necessarily have to do this on a printed form with carbon copies, but you do have to write something.

Your documentation should include what you and your employee have discussed—the successes and problems of the work period. Write, as you have spoken, in behavioral terms. Be specific about what the employee has or has not done. If there have been problems, state that you have discussed them and what you and the employee have agreed to do about them.

Make sure that what you write matches what you and your employee have talked about. One advantage to writing the appraisal and agreements is that if you misunderstood each other, the differences in interpretation will probably come out when you both review the written document.

Some managers are tempted to put into the written document touchy subjects they were unwilling to talk about. This is dishonest and cowardly, especially if the employee will not see the write-up. To avoid this deception, many organizations require that the employee sign the appraisal form. Regardless of what the organization requires, let your employee see what you have written. It may clear up any misunderstandings, and it will be a gesture of openness and trust.

Some managers have their employees write the appraisal themselves; then the manager signs the document. Other managers write their own appraisals, but have their employees write one as well. This gives the employee an opportunity to express an opinion and is especially important when boss and subordinate disagree.

Remember that documentation is important. Written reports of performance appraisal can become legal documents if a decision based on performance is later challenged in court. However, this documentation should be an outgrowth of the discussion, which is still the major purpose of performance appraisal. Some managers get this backward. Because their companies put such emphasis on the "form," it seems as if the form is all-important and the discussion is only incidental. This approach completely misses the point that the major objective is to improve performance.

Summary

- Objectives of the performance appraisal meeting:
  - To learn what the employee thinks
  - To give your own assessment
  - To plan for the next period
- At the beginning of the meeting state the objectives and put the employee at ease.
- Let the employee speak first.
- Listen actively:
  - Listen for emotional and logical content.
  - Summarize and give feedback.
  - Get clarification of points you don't understand.
  - Say what *you think* the speaker is feeling.
- Respond to the self-appraisal. First say what you agree with, then what you disagree with. Then bring up new topics the employee hasn't touched on.
  - *Be supportive.* Use supportive behavior to make the discussion constructive.
  - *Avoid defensiveness.* Avoid criticizing your employee's character and confine your remarks to what the employee has or has not done.
  - *Emphasize mutual problem solving.* Work with your subordinate to come to agreements on what changes, if any, are needed and what course of action will accomplish those changes.
  - *Encourage participation.* Give the employee an opportunity to express the self-appraisal in a receptive atmosphere. This is best accomplished by letting the employee speak first.
  - *Set goals.* Enthusiastic performance improvement efforts are more likely to follow if you end the appraisal meeting with agreement between you and your subordinate on specific goals for the future.
- And performance appraisal has these outcomes:
  - You will learn about the employee's problems and motivations.
  - The employee will learn of your expectations and evaluation.
  - You will both set expectations and leave the meeting with a new plan.

Scripts for Better Communication

Here are some phrases that may help you conduct a smooth performance appraisal interview:

- If the employee has trouble getting started on the self-appraisal:

  "Why don't you start by talking about the XYZ project?" (Pick a topic that the employee will feel comfortable with, a success rather than a failure.)

  "It seems to me the PDQ project was harder than we expected. What's your perspective on that?"

  "I know this sort of thing is hard to do. Start wherever you like. I'm eager to hear what these past six months have been like from your point of view."

- If the employee dwells on one aspect of the self-appraisal:

  "I can see that sales reports presented you with some real challenges. (Summarize what the employee has been saying.) Let's go on now to . . ."

  "Let's write down this problem so we can talk about its solution later. But now, let's go on to . . ."

  "I'm glad you enjoyed working on ABC, Jim. How did DEF go?"

- If the employee "passes the buck":

  "You feel that Jane was really responsible for this problem, Richard, but was there anything you could have done to work around the problem?"

  "I know how hard it is to control work when so many factors are involved. What can you do in the future that will ensure that this won't happen again?"

- If the employee presses to know the salary or promotion implications of the boss's appraisal:

  "I know how important this next raise (or promotion) is to you, Patsy, but that is something I won't decide until after we complete this assessment. Right now let's concentrate on what you've accomplished and what your plan should be for the next period."

Descriptive (Nonevaluative)

Yes: "I think you spent your time on the most important work, like the customer service letters, rather than on trivia. I appreciate that."

No: "You exercised good judgment, Henry."

Problem-Oriented (Noncontrolling)

Yes: "Tom, how can we prevent these double shipments in the future?"

No: "You have to file the green copies as soon as the order is written and check the folder at shipping and at billing time. There's no other way to control this problem."

Spontaneous (Nonstrategic)

Yes: "You feel we can do a spot check rather than a full audit, Lilly. I'm afraid that would mean some mistakes would slip through."

No: "Wouldn't a spot check mean that some mistakes would get by us?"

Equal (Nonsuperior)

Yes: "George, you're relatively new in the unit. That should give you a fresh perspective. I've been around here since the year one and know the place inside out. Between the two of us we should be able to come up with just the procedure for the Memphis office."

No: "In my 12 years in this organization I've learned that special treatment of one field office is impossible."

Empathetic (Nonneutral)

Yes: "Having to make a presentation at the executive committee meeting is a scary proposition. The first time I did it I lost 3 pounds in two days."

No: "Listen, Scott, you'll never get anywhere around here until the executive committee members know who you are."

Provisional (Noncertain)

Yes: "My approach to this would be to visit the Atlanta plant and get on-the-spot observations from the people on the line. What would be your approach, Noel?"

No: "Go to Atlanta and talk to them. That's the way to find out what really happened."

Transactional Analysis Examples

Yes

Adult: "Alice, this project is two weeks behind schedule. What could we have done to bring it in on time?"

Adult: "We should have planned on Frank taking more than two weeks to get his analysis in. And I should have gotten some extra training in how to operate the new computer system."

No

Parent: "Alice, the fact that you let this project get so far behind schedule is a big disappointment to me."

Child: "I can't help it, Claude. Frank's never ready with his part of the analysis. Besides, I've never done anything like this before."

Assertiveness Examples

Yes

Assertive: "Richard, I feel getting the quarterly wage report in on time is more important than cataloging the videotape library."

No

Aggressive: "Richard, only a nincompoop would mess around with videotapes and ignore the quarterly wage report."

Passive: "What happened to the quarterly wage report?"

Chapter 7

Appraisal and the Poor Performer

Managing high performers is usually easy. Mostly they manage themselves. Getting poor performers to improve is the real challenge, and for them performance appraisal is critical. But managers often avoid the emotional hassle involved in confronting the poor performer. This is unfortunate because it takes away the most powerful tool the employee and the manager have for improving the employee's performance.

We have already talked about planning for performance improvement. You know how important follow-up is for the employee whose performance has been below standard. I will not belabor these points. After the planning and follow-up, as you prepare for the appraisal meeting, you may discover that you still have an employee with a problem.

Your first step is to make sure that the employee is a poor performer. Sometimes managers mistakenly identify employees as poor performers because their personalities are not appealing or their methods are unorthodox. A poor performer is simply someone who is not accomplishing the work.

If your employee's level of work consistently falls short of requirements even after those requirements have been made clear and the person has acknowledged them, you need to take special steps to either turn the performance around or move the employee out of the job.

When you analyze the performance of such a person, look for patterns of behavior that might be creating the problem. Where you see such patterns, you should look for their cause. If the cause is something in the work environment, you may need to change it to support the proper behavior and enable the employee to succeed.

The section on assessing performance in Chapter 5 gives a thorough discussion of this kind of analysis. If the cause of the behavior is within the employee, you will have to try to get the employee to change that behavior.

Sometimes, however, the behavior has become part of the employee's personality. If you feel the problem borders on issues of personality, approach with great care. You as a manager represent a business, and it is not within the business's purview to ask employees to change their personalities. Remember that you can ask employees to change only their behavior on the job.

In discussing poor performance, you can expect the employee to respond emotionally. Even though you may practice the supportive behavior techniques outlined in Chapter 6, pointing out a person's poor performance is likely to elicit a defensive response. Your employee may try to protect his or her self-image by denying that the problem exists or by blaming it on someone else. Some people give long explanations for why they behaved as they did. Let the person talk. You want to solve a problem, not take away a person's dignity. Talking may sometimes help employees work off some embarrassment so that they can then think rationally about the issues.

Some employees will agree with criticism very quickly. Before the boss has made the statement, the person is saying, "Yes I know; it's my fault." Sometimes this means that the employee has anticipated the criticism and wants to be saved the embarrassment of hearing it said out loud. That's okay. But sometimes the employee hears the criticism coming, doesn't really understand the problem or agree with the boss's analysis, but acts accepting to avoid the issue or to seem polite or cooperative.

If the employee agrees too quickly with your criticism, especially if the problems didn't come up or were glossed over in the self-appraisal, you have reason to doubt the depth of the person's agreement. It is best to check further. Many times managers are tempted to drop a subject that is making them and the employee anxious. But the first steps to a change in behavior are a conscious acceptance that there is indeed a problem and then an understanding of what it is. All your other efforts will be wasted without this acceptance. Tell your employee that you know this sort of problem is painful to talk about. Say you are happy that the employee wants to agree with your assessment. But then gently ask the person about what he or she thinks the problem is. You don't want to rub salt in your employee's wounds, but you do want to make sure you are getting more than surface acceptance and then go on to make a plan for performance improvement.

Some people say, "I quit." It's rare to have an employee quit on the spot when faced with criticism, but some do. You may be tempted to say, "That's fine with me." Don't. Ask the employee to think it over for a while and proceed with your "rescue efforts." Accepting a resignation under such circumstances can create other problems later. The employee could decide that he or she was really forced to quit under duress and may file a complaint, a grievance with the union, or take some other legal action. At the very least it will make performance appraisal interviews look dangerous to other employees.

When you plan an appraisal meeting with a problem employee, you need to assess whether the employee is really trying. Your approach to someone who is working very hard and still not achieving objectives will differ from your approach to someone whose failure is the result of an apparent lack of motivation.

If the Employee Is Trying but Failing

Even if you have planned and followed up, the first things to check are whether the employee really understood what was required and if the person was properly trained. If the problem was one of unclear expectations, it is as much your failure as it is the employee's. Go back and start over, but this time put the emphasis on clear communication and frequent follow-up. Plan another formal review soon so the situation doesn't get out of hand. Another failure of this sort will mean greater losses both for the organization because of work that doesn't get done and for the employee because of the loss of self-respect.

Sometimes a person is working hard but is unable to tell how successful those efforts are. If the failure occurred because the employee went off course and didn't know it, you need to invent ways for the person to get immediate feedback—warning systems to help the person stay on track, copies of reports that inform the employee of the status of the work. You may have to spend more time coaching and counseling until the employee is able to see the warning signs.

Again we return to the question: Is the job doable? In a client company of mine three of the last four incumbents in a certain job have been fired for incompetence. I suggested that before anyone else suffer needlessly they should look at the design of the job and its place in the organization. Don't let three out of four people in your unit fail before you make the necessary changes. Chapter 4 gives a more thorough discussion of the reasons why people fail and what to do in each case.

You may have a situation where there is nothing intrinsically wrong with the job, but where the incumbent is just incapable of doing it. If you have a person who has been working hard (remember that is our assumption in this part of the discussion), you will want to try to keep that person if you can. You may have to find ways to redesign the job so that the person can do it. This sort of juggling is easier if you are working on a unique job. If seven or eight people who work for you are all doing the same job, it's going to be hard to change it for one person without changing it for everyone. Changes that make it easier for the person with the problem may make it necessary to change the salary rating to comply with equal pay for equal work laws. Besides, you can't make things simpler for one person; the others will resent the inequity. But if you can find ways of doing the job that emphasize the incumbent's strengths rather than weaknesses, you may be able to save a hardworking employee. Your flexibility may even serve to increase the person's already high level of motivation.

If after trying to save the incumbent, you find there is no way to match the job to the person, you may have to move the person out of the job. When skill or knowledge, not motivation, is the employee's problem, you should try to find another job for the person in the organization. If you have to ask the person to leave the firm, make sure that you follow the rules for termination given later in this chapter. Stretch the rules on severance benefits as much as you can. Show the departing employee and those who remain that you are a manager who appreciates effort.

If the Employee Isn't Even Trying

Little else can discourage a manager more than working with a person who doesn't even seem to try. We come here to the subject of human motivation—a mystery that itself has been the subject of many books. We will not take it up in depth here. If you are one of the many managers who struggle with the question of how you can motivate your people, the answer is simple, you can't. You can only draw out (or turn off) motivation that is already there. The planning, the follow-up, and the encouragement described in the last few chapters are designed to draw out the employee's motivation. If they haven't worked, you may be up against a more fundamental problem.

One possible reason for your employees' lack of effort may be that they do not respect your opinion of what is required. I know this can seem ludicrous; after all, you are the boss. But sometimes employees don't accept the boss's evaluation of what is needed in the job. This is more likely to happen if the employee is older, has more experience in the field, or has worked for the firm longer than the boss. Sometimes your employee feels he should have gotten your job. Resentment against those who appointed you will sometimes be aimed at you instead. This may cause the shortsighted response of not doing the work. If you feel this is the case, you are best advised to get the issue out in the open. Use the techniques of supportive communication. Sit with the person and say, "Ray, I know that you have been in the department longer than I have, and I would imagine that might make it hard to accept my appointment as manager." Draw out the person's feelings; don't try to establish your authority without showing respect for your employee's knowledge and feelings.

The employees' lack of effort may stem from the fact that the goals you set together are not appealing to them or that they don't see enough of a reward (or punishment) to make the effort worthwhile. If you can somehow help employees identify their own goals and if these goals can be made to mesh with the organization's goals, you may be able to draw out motivation to achieve the work. People work best if they feel their work is somehow meeting a need for them. These needs go far beyond the need to support themselves. People work to learn, for a challenge, for the social contact, to have a feeling of independence and so on. The more you know about your employees' needs, the better you will be able to draw out their motivations.

Remember that your job is to get the job done, not to mold your employees' characters. You should lay out the options and let employees make the choices. You aren't going to have much success trying to get people to do things they really don't want to do. Frequently what works best is to focus on employee strengths and find ways these assets can lead to personal success. By looking at the positive side, you may be able to bring out the best in a person. At the very least you need to make clear that the person's choices are to do the job or to move to another job. Then you can leave the choice up to the employee. As long as a lackadaisical employee feels poor performance can continue with impunity, it's doubtful you will see any improvement.

If the employee displays a sincere willingness to change, the way is clear.

Define the Problem

Be as specific as you can in stating the difference between acceptable and unacceptable performance. The best approach is to have the employee do as much of this as possible.

Pinpoint the Needed Changes

Describe as accurately as you can what the employee should do instead.

Arrange for Feedback

Figure out how the employee will learn if he or she is succeeding. This will be critical to the behavior change. Of course, some of the feedback will come from you, but it would be good if it could also come from others, and it would be even better if it could somehow be incorporated into the work routine.

Express Confidence

Your plan won't work if your employee senses that you feel it can't. You must let the employee know that you feel success is possible and that you expect the plan to work.

Tie Consequences to Performance

Success in this change effort should bring some reward; failure, some adverse consequence. Tell your employee what these will be.

When you are developing the how-to's, come up with several different ways of solving the problem. See if your employee can invent a plan or a new pattern of behavior that will work better. If you define the way you want the person to act too narrowly, you may make the change too difficult. Sometimes you need to accept improvement in steps. Don't expect the person to make major changes quickly, especially if you are dealing with entrenched habits.

What Do You Do If Nothing Works?

"They don't know how to say get out . . . so they create a situation you can't work in, you finally can't live in—tension, abuse, mostly subtle, sometimes violent. Chip away at your pride, your security, until you begin to doubt, then fear. . . . Ramsey wants me to resign. . . . He thinks he can make me miserable enough to do that." These lines are from the 1955 television play *Patterns* by Rod Serling. Organizations are frequently at their most inhumane when they want to get rid of someone. Managers often do force people out instead of facing the tough task and asking them to leave in some humane way. Some managers will do anything to avoid firing people, even make them so uncomfortable that they finally resign. We need to learn to avoid this unnecessary cruelty.

But firing people seems inevitable; we can minimize how often we have to do it, but we will all have to do it sometime. We need to learn to do it in the most humane way possible, both for the boss and the subordinate.

If you are thinking of firing someone, let me ask you to pause for reflection. You are about to put yourself in a very uncomfortable position to say nothing of the fact that you are going to do something that may profoundly influence someone else's life. Don't do it unless you are sure you are doing the right thing. Ask yourself one more time if your expectations of the person are reasonable. If you are a perfectionist you may be demanding a level of performance that is impossible. It may help you put things in perspective if you think about your chances of finding someone who will do the job better. Some jobs lack the intrinsic rewards that will motivate a person to high levels of performance. If you can't change the job and you can't get anyone to do it really well, you may have to settle for less than perfect work.

If you have tried the advice given so far in this chapter and not gotten the desired results, you may have to face the fact that your employee cannot or will not change. In that case, you may have to remove the person from the job. If the problem is that an otherwise good employee is just incapable of performing the required tasks, your first solution should be to try transferring the person to another job that the person can do. Open as many doors within the organization as you can before you ask a hardworking person to leave. But be careful about transferring people. Do not palm off your problems on other supervisors. This is a common way of dealing with a distasteful job. Rather than going through the pain of getting the person off the payroll altogether, some managers will just get the person transferred out of the department and let someone else deal with the problem. This hurts the company and the employee. For the company the loss is obvious. For the employee, it just postpones the time when he or she will have to face the fact of having chosen the wrong field or having unrealistic expectations. If people are going to correct their thinking and learn to manage their lives happily and productively, it is better if they face these realities earlier than later. Besides, if you take the coward's way out, other managers will get the idea that you recommend the wrong people for transfer. This will destroy your credibility.

I know, the very thought of firing a person makes you nervous, but that's good. That reluctance keeps many of us from treating people like disposable pieces of equipment. On the other hand, if we have to do it sometimes, we should understand our feelings about it. Most managers feel sorry for the person. It makes them feel bad to have to inflict pain on someone. We also feel a certain amount of guilt about our roles in the failure. We may have not given the person the necessary managerial support. We may have picked the wrong person for the job or misrepresented it to the person at hiring time. We also know that letting someone go can have a disastrous effect on the morale of those who stay, especially if our action seems unfair to the other employees.

It is true that firing a person can be a destructive act. But its destructiveness can be kept in check. Besides, when faced with being fired as the ultimate consequence, some poor performers may improve. There have been last minute turnarounds that have saved a person's job.

This emphatically does not mean that you should ever threaten anyone in hopes of improving his or her performance. A warning of possible termination should be just that—a warning. If from the beginning the review process is aimed at helping the employee succeed and if termination is the last resort when all attempts at improving the employee's performance have been exhausted, then this step will leave the manager feeling less guilty and leave other employees less demoralized. As for the person being fired, I wish I could say this method would be painless. I don't think this is possible. But we can try to minimize the ego damage. The employee will leave having failed, but should not feel worthless or like a complete failure.

I am speaking here about terminations that result from poor performance, not from layoffs or staff cuts that have to do with poor business performance. These are different, and everyone knows it. Employees who are asked to leave can be told in truth that it is no fault of their own. They are often given generous severance pay or time to look for another job. They still need ego support, but usually being let go in a layoff that involves many people is not as devastating as being the only person who is fired. Unfortunately, layoffs are frequently more devastating than they need to be because they often come as a shock. Following a merger or reorganization, executives will swear that there will be no jobs lost. Woe to those who believe this. They may rest secure one moment only to suddenly find themselves out of a job.

There are some times when results of performance appraisal are used to determine who goes and who stays in a staff reduction. In cases like this, it is most important that the information from the performance appraisal system be reliable and accurate and used fairly. Otherwise we can face legal problems. We may have to show that the system used was a valid one. A later chapter on performance appraisal and the law will explain what it takes to be "legal." At the very least, distrust of the performance appraisal system may result when it is used for what look like punitive purposes.

With All the Legal Restrictions, Is Termination Still Possible?

The mere mention of legal problems in relation to performance appraisal brings up the possibility of lawsuits and how that discourages some managers from firing anyone who belongs to a protected class, that is, minorities, women, handicapped persons, people over forty, and veterans of the Vietnam war. The antidiscrimination laws are needed to protect people who were treated unfairly in the past. But these laws don't mean you can't fire a person in one of these categories. They merely mean that you can't do it without just cause and fair warning. I have seen employers hang onto people who are classified in one of these categories, people whose performance was practically nonexistent, because they were afraid of a lawsuit. The result was wasted corporate dollars and a great loss of morale among members of the staff who had been trying to do their jobs.

In the past, the rule was that an employer could fire a person at will. No one had any protection, and no explanations were necessary. But social changes have made this view inconsistent with modern thinking. With the overwhelming majority of citizens dependent on others for their livelihood, this rule leaves too many people feeling vulnerable. Although union members have contract protections and others are protected by equal opportunity laws, there are still millions of workers who ostensibly could be fired for no reason after years of loyal service.

But the employee rights of protected groups seem to be spreading to all employees. The changes of the past 50 years seem to be doing away with the old master-servant relationship. We see more and more court cases challenging the common law of "termination at will," and many recent decisions extend protection to all employees. It is unlikely that new laws will be passed to give all workers "property rights" to their jobs, but there is enough sentiment in that direction to make it difficult for managers to avoid the issue, especially for long-service employees. As with many issues that have been mandated by law in the past several years, this trend to termination only with just cause makes good business sense. Rather than resist it, employers might do well to embrace it for its good effects on employee morale, loyalty, and commitment. It seems as if we, willingly or not, are all going to be expected to develop objective standards of performance so we can state our "just cause" when we fire someone. The techniques of performance planning, follow-up, and appraisal are a way of establishing such standards. Then we need to follow fair termination procedures.

The Termination Process

Many companies are adopting procedures that ensure "due process" in the case of terminations. Some, like IBM, have an open-door policy: Anyone being terminated or anyone who feels the company's treatment has been unfair can talk to a top executive who must investigate the problem. Certainly, unions will file a grievance and represent a member at a hearing when they feel someone has been fired without just cause. Some companies, sometimes to avoid unionization attempts, have set up internal review boards for cases where the fairness of termination or other personnel actions is questioned. In many companies the human resources department must review any terminations to make sure the organization is not left vulnerable to a lawsuit. If you work for a large organization, there is likely to be some policy for handling terminations and employee grievances. Your first step should be to find out what that policy is.

Regardless of what policy your organization follows, the decision to terminate the employee will begin with you. Some people are fired for obvious and easily provable reasons: they have violated some important rule by fighting, stealing, giving privileged information to competitors, and so on. If such an incident is provable, you won't have any trouble. You should still follow the company policy and file whatever reports are necessary, but you probably won't lose any sleep over firing someone for such a gross infraction.

Absenteeism is another major cause of termination. Sometimes it is used as an excuse when poor performance is really the issue. Other problems are harder to document and prove, so absenteeism becomes the issue. If you are going to fire someone for staying off the job too often, you must have documentation not only that the person was actually absent but that you took steps to try to correct the problem and that you warned the employee that his or her job was in jeopardy. You can't allow people to be late or absent for a long time, say nothing to them about it, and then fire them for it.

Insurbordination is sometimes claimed as the reason for termination. This is a tough issue. We certainly cannot have people around who are constantly challenging our authority in a disruptive way, but we can't expect blind obedience either. Unless you can show that the employee flatly refused to follow some important order, you may not have a case. This is especially true with unionized employees whose rights to stop work as a group are protected by the National Labor-Management Relations Act.

Alcoholism used to be given as a reason for termination, and it still can be, I suppose. However, since many people now view alcoholism as an illness rather than as a character defect, dismissal for drinking can be tricky. It is best to work with experts on this problem. You certainly don't need to keep an employee if the person is drunk on the job, but it would probably be best to treat this as a personal problem rather than as an insult to authority.

This brings us to the most basic reason for dismissal: poor performance. If you have followed our process of work planning, follow-up, and review, you will have the necessary information to show that your judgment of poor performance is based on a job-related standard and was arrived at fairly.

When you feel you have to fire someone, start working on the problem right away. As with most distasteful tasks, we have a tendency to procrastinate. You may daydream about the employee's leaving on his or her own. That sometimes happens, but you can't solve the problem by putting it off. Besides if you wait too long, you will let the person's poor performance seem acceptable, not only to the employee in question but also to others in your group. Start the process before your anxieties build up. Here's what you will do (remember to write and file a report at each step so you will have the proper documentation if you need it later):

- Counsel the person.
- Give a final warning.
- Terminate.

Begin by telling the person that his job is in jeopardy because of poor performance. Make sure that you say this straightforwardly so there is no doubt in the person's mind. You need not be brutal about it, but if you are too vague, the person may not understand the seriousness of what you are saying. Many times managers bungle this first message so that employees later believe that they are being terminated without warning.

This first meeting does not have to be all negative, however. Explain what changes the person has to make to save his job. Put a time limit on the change. Don't make the timing too short in this first step. People need time to change old habits. Two or three months is a typical span between the first warning and the next step. Once you have held this first meeting, write up what was said and file it. Some company policies require that the employee receive a copy of the documentation.

Sometimes after warning a person that dismissal is possible, the manager will avoid the employee because of embarrassment about facing the person. If your efforts to save the person are sincere, you will do just the opposite. Stay in close touch. Encourage the employee; say what your interim observations are; make sure you share any information that will help the person overcome the problem. When the time is up, review the case again.

If the needed improvement hasn't been achieved, you will need to meet the person again. This time have a written warning ready. Address the memo to the employee, state the problem, explain that you met with the person months ago to discuss it and that there has not been sufficient improvement. The note must state that you are warning the person that if the performance doesn't improve in a specified period, you will have to dismiss him. The memo should be unequivocal and so should your statements at the meeting. But again your tone need not be harsh. You can say that you had hoped you wouldn't have to do this and that you hope in the time left the employee will improve his performance and make termination unnecessary. Put a copy of your memo in your own files. Your company policy may also require that you file a copy of the memo with your boss or the personnel department. The time between this written warning and the final decision should be kept fairly short. There is no point in prolonging the agony. One month or even two weeks may be sufficient depending on the nature of the job and the employee's length of service.

Again, do what you can to help the employee improve. Make sure that you observe carefully what is happening. If you avoid the person because of your own discomfort, you can miss important aspects of performance at a critical time. This means that you could come to the wrong decision at the point of final assessment.

What Do You Say after You Say, "You're Fired"?

If, when you make the final appraisal, the necessary improvement is still lacking, tell the person what your judgment is and that you must ask him to leave. This should come as no shock. Once the word is out, you may have to allow the person to let off some steam. You will not change your mind, of course, but you may have to let the person get over some embarrassment. You may even need to break the news and set another meeting where you will discuss the ground rules for the period between the meeting and the person's last day on the job.

At some point you will have to establish when that last day will be, inform the employee of any termination benefits, and explain how the transition will take place. You may want to explain to the employee what you will tell his fellow workers and what you will say to prospective employers. You should try to end this meeting on a positive note. Tell the person that you don't think this failure means he cannot succeed in the future. Emphasize what you think are the person's strong points and what he has to bring to the next job. The person should not leave the meeting feeling worthless.

Some companies have one procedure for firing exempt employees and another for nonexempts. I think the same procedure should apply to both. Usually the procedure for nonexempt employees is the more formal and careful. Executives are not always accorded the same due process as other workers. On the other hand, executives are sometimes kept on the payroll long after they have stopped earning their salaries. My vote is for everyone to be treated with equal fairness.

Some Reminders

Regardless of the reasons for termination, your job as a manager is to get the employee to accept the problem. I know of one unbelievable instance where over a year after an executive was "fired" she was still on the payroll because no one could face getting her to accept the dismissal. Getting an employee to understand and accept what's going on and to proceed peacefully with the process of leaving and finding another job depends on a number of things—the amount of severance pay, the period of time given to look for a new job, and especially whether the manager has treated the employee with respect. If the employee feels insulted or robbed of dignity, there is more likely to be trouble. If the manager is concerned and humane, the employee may not feel it necessary to take extraordinary measures to defend his or her rights.

Your tone in discussing all the issues related to termination should be forthright and honest, but aimed at preserving the employee's self-respect and confidence. You may have to listen to rationalizations and complaints. Don't argue back. It is better to say, "I understand how difficult this sort of thing is to take" and to help the employee think about how to use his or her strengths to succeed in the future. If you try to remove all of a person's defenses, you will only make trouble for the employee and maybe for yourself and the firm. Tact is, I guess, what I am recommending. It should be a part of every manager's repertory. One way to show some humanity is to take your time to thoroughly discuss the issue. You may be tempted to rush through a painful discussion. Give your employee all the time needed. Allow the person time to react emotionally—don't expect an angry, upset person to discuss performance rationally. No matter what happens, remember there is no room in a termination discussion for rudeness or sarcasm from the manager. Adding insult to injury has always been a bad idea.

Protecting the Organization

Many organizations are aware that a person who has just been fired might want to retaliate and many are in a position to do so. If the person is allowed to continue at work, sabotage may be possible. To prevent this, people in sensitive jobs, who have access to confidential information, are sometimes asked to leave the premises immediately. Some companies do this as a matter of policy. Others decide on an individual basis whether there is any real danger in allowing the person normal access to the work area and a reasonable transition period before leaving. If you don't know the person well enough to know how to handle this, you probably don't know him well enough to be firing him.

Always be sure to document what you discuss at meetings concerning termination. After each meeting, even this last one, summarize what you and the employee have said and file these minutes in case, later on, you need to review exactly what was said.

References

Some managers will discuss at termination time what they intend to tell prospective employers. They work with the employee to arrive at a "story" that is acceptable to both of them.

Treat references for a fired employee with caution. Former employees can sue if you give them a negative reference. The law says that such a reference must contain false and defamatory statements for the employee to have a case. But it is still best to be cautious, especially about what you write. Some personnel departments have rules against giving any negative references, even if they are true and provable. Some will answer questions over the phone, but refuse to put anything in writing. Even if you can successfully defend your company from a defamation suit, it may not be worth risking one. They are expensive.

Besides, we have said that failing in the job you provided does not mean the employee will not be able to succeed in a different environment. Unless the employee has done something violent or dishonest, there is no reason for you to spoil the person's chances elsewhere. If you are still feeling vindictive, even after the person is gone, you ought to ask yourself why. And perhaps look for a more productive way to use your energy.

Summary

- Managers sometimes mistakenly label people whose methods are unorthodox as poor performers.
- Sometimes the work environment or the job design prevents the employee from doing the work.
- Remember your job is to get the poor performer to change job-related behavior, not personality.
- If necessary, let the employee blow off steam before you try to discuss the problem rationally.
- If the employee seems to agree with everything too quickly, make sure that he or she really understands and agrees with your definition of the problem.

- If the employee quits, don't accept the resignation on the spot. Let the employee think it over.
- If the employee is trying hard but still failing:
  - Make sure that the failure isn't caused by lack of understanding of what's needed or impossibility of the task.
  - Consider changing the job to conform to the abilities of your highly motivated, but unsuccessful, employee.
  - Transfer the hardworking employee to another job in the company.
  - Terminate the employee only as a last resort.
- If the employee isn't even trying, try to turn the person around:
  - Define the problem.
  - Pinpoint the needed changes.
  - Arrange for feedback.
  - Express confidence.
  - Tie consequences to performance.
- Fire an employee only for job-related reasons—poor performance, bad attendance record, misconduct on the job, and so forth.
- Always document all decisions and discussions involving disciplinary action, especially those that may lead to termination.
- If you must fire someone:
  - Counsel the person. Say what specific behavior must change and state unequivocally that the person's job is in jeopardy.
  - Give a final warning if you don't get the needed improvement.
  - Terminate. Inform the employee of how the termination will be handled—severance pay, last day of work, and so on.
- In any disciplinary action:
  - Allow the employee to talk out his or her feelings.
  - Be firm, but don't argue.
  - Help the employee get over *this* failure by talking about what strengths the person has to bring to another job.
  - Protect the interests of the company from possible sabotage if necessary.
- To avoid legal problems, don't write negative references unless you have proof of the employee's wrongdoing.

Chapter 8

Solving Performance Appraisal Problems

Regardless of how well you follow the advice of this book so far, there will still be instances where performance appraisal raises difficulties. There will still be groups or individuals who need special attention or whose concerns may be different from those of most employees.

First of all, any widespread problems with performance appraisal may just be symptoms of other managerial problems. The manager who finds it impossible to do performance planning and appraisal and make it productive may be working in a company that has other pervasive problems that doom this attempt at good management. In such a case, all the managers in the company will have problems with performance appraisal, or at least all of those who try to do it.

Where a company's success with performance appraisal is spotty, something serious is wrong. It may be something as simple as the performance appraisal system itself. Perhaps the system is cumbersome or inappropriate. Perhaps the managers who are trying to use the system don't have the skills they need to make performance appraisal succeed. Or there may be a basic problem with the management of the organization. Perhaps the structure of the company is such that jobs are not clearly delineated or responsibilities and authority are not clearly defined. If this kind of basic problem exists, it will be nearly impossible for performance planning and appraisal to work as we have outlined it here. In fact, attempting to plan as outlined in Chapter 3 will point up the problem because the planning process will uncover all the uncertainties about who is supposed to do what and who reports to whom. In such a case, the management has no choice but to organize the staff to do the work first and then to proceed with planning and appraisal. In other words, the more basic problems of organization, structure, and mission must be solved before the performance planning and appraisal system can be effective. You have to decide what you are managing and why you are managing it before you can decide how to manage it, which is really the subject of this book.

Individual managers whose attempts at performance planning and appraisal end in failure may have a problem in managerial style. Their own ambition or dedication to getting the job done may be clouding their judgment and make them insensitive to the real feelings of their people. They may be creating a climate of fear in which any attempt at performance appraisal may seem threatening. If your subordinates, even the best ones, seem threatened by the prospect of performance appraisal, you may need to examine your own managerial style to see if it is hindering you as a manager.

Employees will also react negatively to performance appraisal by managers whose opinions they do not respect. For instance, a manager of a technical area who is not an expert in the subject may not have the credibility needed to judge the work. Managers who are given charge of areas they do not thoroughly understand need to attend to their own knowledge gaps and lack of credibility first. I think it's best to confront the issue by admitting the lack of technical knowledge. Rather than trying to fake it, sit down with your people individually and say, "You are the expert in this subject; I am going to rely on you to help me plan the work and understand your concerns. I will be able to support you by . . ." Then fill in with what you have to bring to the party: knowledge of the company as a whole, clout with upper management, and so on. Don't abdicate or apologize for your role, but define subtly why a person without technical expertise has been put in charge. By beginning the discussion with expressions of respect for the employee's superior technical knowledge, you can alleviate some of the hostility your employee may feel.

What to Do If the Employee Says, "No Fair"

Sometimes, the meetings are held, the planning and follow-up is done, the appraisal meeting is held, and when the boss writes up the appraisal for the file, the employee still thinks it's unfair. Usually this problem is a result of disagreement between boss and subordinate about what the job entails or what is important. It can also result from sloppy planning, especially from work plans that are vague about outcomes. There should have been plenty of opportunities to clear this up during interim follow-up meetings, but if the appraisal is written and the employee still has a grievance, you will have to deal with it.

First of all listen to the employee's complaint. Treat the employee's feelings with respect. You can sympathize with a person's feelings without expressing agreement with his or her ideas. Avoid defensiveness or loudly explaining why your point of view is correct. Allow the employee to ventilate and then pursue whatever avenues are available to redress the grievance. If you are confident in your conclusions, this won't cause you any problems. If you are not confident in your conclusions, then why did you write them down with such certainty?

Where unions are involved, there may be a formal grievance procedure that the employee can follow. Some nonunion companies, particularly those that are trying to avoid unionization, have grievance procedures similar to those instituted through union contracts. Most of these involve a series of appeal steps, usually beginning with the boss's boss and going up the chain of command or going to a personnel representative whose job it is to redress employee grievances. Some companies use an ombudsman, an executive appointed to investigate and redress all employee grievances.

Even if your company does not have a grievance policy, if you have carried out the appraisal in good faith, you should allow the employee to talk over the problem with your boss or someone in the personnel department. If you allow people to carry their complaints to others who can give them a fair hearing, you will show that you are trying to be honest and fair. If you sit on people who complain, you will seem like a person who has something to hide.

Some procedures also allow the employee to write a reply to the manager's appraisal and put that in the file. When the manager and the employee differ strongly in their views of performance, it is a good idea to let the comments of both be filed together. This gives both parties a voice when the file is reviewed for future decisions.

Some managers try to avoid the whole issue of the fairness of their appraisals by not showing the employee what they have written. They will have the review meeting and then write something that is substantially different from what they have discussed. In this way, by deception, they hope to avoid confrontation. This has always seemed to me to be a useless approach. What good is it to let employees think they are doing well when the opposite is the case? There would certainly be no spur to performance improvement in such a case. The employee whose performance was really below standard would eventually get the message when no raises were forthcoming. The only thing I can think of is that it would prevent the firm from considering the person for a promotion. And in a case like that, the message would eventually get through anyway. If you are inclined to say one thing and write another, you should really ask yourself why. It may be that you lack the communications skills to get the negatives across without hurting the person's feelings.

To prevent the write-one-thing–say-another deception, many companies have a policy of having the employee sign the performance appraisal form. This signature does not usually indicate agreement with the assessment, but just indicates that the employee has seen the form. Some employees, notably those who work in federal, state, and municipal agencies have the legal right to review their own files, and in some states they may even have the right to write corrections of what they consider false statements in the record. Employees of private companies have very little legal protection in this regard, but again some companies have special policies that grant their employees the same rights to review their own files. You should check to see what laws and procedures apply in your case. Again, I find that openness with employees pays dividends in terms of morale and enthusiasm. (A later chapter on the legal aspects of performance appraisal gives more details on the rights of employees to review and correct their own employment records.)

Appraising Older Workers

Our work force, like our population, is getting older. The demographers tell us that we cannot expect to easily replace all our older workers with younger ones. This will be true especially in instances where a firm requires people with rare skills.

People will also have to stay on the job longer to support themselves. It has become impossible for the Social Security system and other pension plans to support people for the 15 to 20 years they can expect to live beyond age 65. In the past, our society has told people that if they worked to age 60 or 65, they could have a paid vacation for the rest of their lives. This is no longer economically feasible. And increasingly, it isn't considered desirable. Many people fear that idleness will injure the good health they hope to enjoy in their old age. There have also been changes in the law; we now have laws to prevent discrimination against older workers.

Most companies are totally unprepared to deal with the aging of the work force. In the past, and still to a great extent even today, their way of dealing with older workers was to sweeten the retirement pot and get them out of the way through early retirement. If this didn't work, companies had mandatory retirement at age 65 to fall back on. We no longer have mandatory retirement, and it is becoming clearer to older workers that early retirement, even with special benefits packages, is not feasible. A healthy woman of 55 can expect to live another 30 years. The prospect of giving up a career with 30 years more to live is not reasonable to most people. We must learn to manage people to keep them productive until they are really ready for retirement.

First, be sure that you don't break the law. To comply with the nondiscrimination laws, never base an employment decision on the employee's age. Never make assumptions about how the person's age would affect his or her decisions, ambition, mental capacities, and so on. Never do anything that could be misinterpreted as coercion to retire. Before age 70, retirement must be a totally voluntary decision. (As of this writing, mandatory retirement at age 70 is still possible, except for all federal and some other protected employees. But even this may be changed. Soon all mandatory retirement may be abolished.)

If you need to know what the employee's plans are, it is fair to ask, but you should ask the question in an innocuous way. For instance, you might say, "Tell me how you feel about your career at this point in your life," and "Why do you feel that way?" Neutral questions like these will allow the employee to bring up the subject of age, a question which we know can be a touchy one. Then you can go on to discuss the employee's needs and the firm's needs and do your planning.

Sometimes older workers present a special problem for younger managers. When your employee is older than you, each of you may misinterpret the other's actions. Managers often assume that older workers will be difficult to manage, that they will resent being told what to do by a younger person. Older workers sometimes are resentful of younger managers; they may feel that their longer experience better qualifies them for the managerial job. Sometimes they feel passed over, like has-beens in an organization they have served for many years. Sometimes the employee who feels passed over transfers anger at the decision makers to the person who got the management job—you.

It is best to confront this issue head on. Please notice that I said confront the issue, not the person. Sit down with your employee and state the problem. "Martin, I can imagine if I had your years of experience, I would resent being passed over for promotion in favor of someone with less experience in the department. I didn't make the decision to put myself in this job, but I'm glad I got the job, and I'm going to do my best to see that everyone here is treated fairly and rewarded for good performance." Let the person know that you respect his superior knowledge or experience. "You know this place inside and out. I need you. I know what our company looks like from the customer's point of view, since I used to work for one of our customers. Together we should make a dynamite team. I hope we can find productive ways to work together." Again your job is not to apologize for being the manager, it is to help the employee get past the initial hurt and to set the relationship on a productive footing: to establish your authority as a manager without tramping all over the employee's already injured self-esteem.

Self-esteem may become a particularly sensitive point for some workers about the age of 55. Research shows that about this age many people begin to perceive an ebbing of their influence in the organization. They also sometimes begin to get signals from the organization that they are less valued. Although at age 55, most employees have 10 to 15 work years left, only one in a thousand gets a promotion after age 55. The conscious or subconscious realization that the next 10 years may be a dead end can be devastating. This comes at a time when these people may be facing other indications that their roles are changing. Ninety-five percent of people age 55 no longer have children at home. Their roles as nurturers, creators, movers, and shakers seem to be over.

Most people at this age must assume roles as conservators and mentors. They must train those who will shape the future without being shapers of that future themselves. This can be a bitter pill. It isn't that this role is not an important one. It is critical. The problem is that our society has traditionally undervalued it. Therefore people facing this transition often dread it. This can make performance planning and appraisal especially difficult for a time. You will have to treat employees who are facing this problem gently. First of all don't bring up the issue yourself. Just because someone is about 55 years old doesn't mean the person is ready to make this transition. Many people remain ambitious and highly productive well past this age. You need to proceed with planning as you would with any other employee. If you detect trouble, it is not a bad idea to try to bring out its cause. Don't suggest what you think the cause is. Say something like, "I have a sense that you are upset by the work plan we've come up with." Let the employee raise the concern about age and role in the organization. Then go on to deal with the issues.

There is a time when it is fair to raise the question of retirement. This is when an employee nears age 65. Since this has been "normal" retirement age for about a century, it is tied in with many things. Employee benefits packages and social security are still geared to retirement at age 65. There are Medicare and other senior citizen benefits to deal with. As your employee nears this age, you will want to bring this up in the planning process. Don't come across as suggesting that it's time to go. Just talk about whatever choices and new benefits the employee needs to understand.

When the employee has made the decision to retire, you can begin to plan ways to make the transition easy for the group and the employee. Often, more experienced workers are walking around with a wealth of information in their heads. One objective for an employee who has decided to retire might be to pass this knowledge along by preparing procedures manuals or by instructing others in the skills and knowledge gained over the years.

Real problems can arise when an older employee doesn't realize that he or she is no longer capable of doing the job. I don't mean here that we would prefer to have a younger person. Pushing out older workers just because we want someone younger in the job is not only unfair and often cruel, it's illegal. My point here is that sometimes people are no longer mentally or physically capable of doing the job and don't realize it. The National Council on Aging has devised GULHEMP, a series of capacity measurement tests, to evaluate capability. These might be worth investigating if you are looking for ways to find out whether capability is the problem.

Basically, you will follow the performance planning and appraisal cycle with all of your people including those who are nearing retirement. Just keep in mind the special considerations mentioned here as you go along.

What about
the Self-Motivated Superstar?

How, you may wonder, can such a person need special attention when most of the time "special attention" implies a problem. Although most managers would do well to spend a lot of time and energy focusing on their best performers, the opposite often happens. You may work hard with weaker employees trying to help them improve. This is necessary and good, but it should not be done at the expense of your successful people. Keeping them performing at high levels, in fact keeping them at all, may depend on how you treat them. Of course there are some rare people who will continue to perform at the highest levels no matter what anyone else does. You could assume that your best workers fall into this category. But you wouldn't know if you were wrong until it was too late. Better to make the effort to maintain the high performance. Here's how:

Be Generous with Rewards

Do this not only with raises and promotions but also with other tangible and intangible rewards. Some companies have bonus and stock option plans. Some people are into status symbols—nice offices, company cars, and so on. Just about everyone responds to recognition, public and private. Announcements and public thank-yous are helpful. So are reminders that you appreciate the person's contribution. Follow the rules for giving good compliments outlined in Chapter 5. Depending on the employee and the company rules, you may be able to give people extra time off, flexibility in schedules, trips to the annual sales meeting. Make sure that what you offer as a reward is really something the employee will find rewarding.

Find Out Why
the Person Works So Hard

Many managers want to know what will motivate the lax employee, but few bother to ask what makes the hard worker run. When you review performance with your best people, ask them, "What rewards do you get from doing your job so well?" You may not get the full answer, because sometimes people themselves don't realize why, but you may hear things about what needs the person is satisfying by working so hard. You can then make sure that the job continues to satisfy those needs so the high performance will continue.

You can also avoid "rewarding" the person with things that are the opposite of what's wanted or needed. A person who is working to forget some personal problem doesn't want to be rewarded with time off. Assignments that are even more challenging may be the best reward. A person who is striving for status and its symbols may not want a higher level job if it means leaving the home office for the boonies. In other words, find out what rewards will best match the employee's needs.

Keep the Person Growing

Regardless of how wonderful your employee is, no one is perfect. Even your best employee can still learn and grow. Don't forget to plan for challenge and growth with your best people. Frequently the excellent employees are the ones most interested in growth and development. If they get only compliments and rewards, they may come to think that there is no room for growth in the job, and they may leave.

What If They Want a Raise or Promotion that Isn't Possible?

The closest thing I've ever come to a formula for explaining human behavior is this equation

$$R - E = H \text{ or } (F)$$

where R stands for reality, E for expectations, H for happiness, and F for frustration. The formula states that we take reality and subtract from it our expectations. If reality is greater than our expectations, we are happy. If our expectations are greater than what we wind up getting, we have a negative result, frustration.

Many times when employees are upset with the size of a raise or with the promotion opportunities, it is because they have somehow come to expect more than they are getting. Their expectations can arise from something as uncontrollable as wishful thinking, but frequently those expectations are based on their own past experience, discussions with other employees, or guesses about what others are getting in raises. You may also be the culprit. In trying to sell a job to a prospective employee, managers sometimes give the opportunities available a big buildup. Sometimes we use vague promises of big rewards to get people to perform at their highest levels. People can't think about vague ideas for long without trying to translate them into something more concrete. The boss says, "Do this job well for me, Carl, and I'll see that you are well taken care of." The employee immediately starts to imagine what he will get. Suddenly, "well taken care of" becomes a 15 percent raise, an immediate promotion to assistant manager, or a chair on the executive committee. Then when the "promised" reward is not forthcoming, the manager has to deal with a frustrated employee. There are better ways.

First of all, being specific will help. If you must refer to possible rewards, say, if you can, exactly what they will be. If you aren't sure, give a range. Tell the person under what circumstances the promotion or raise will be awarded. *Stress* that you are not making a promise.

In other words, you can avoid causing frustration in your employees by not raising unrealistic expectations. Remember (How could you forget?) that most managers have responsibility but not total authority. Increases and promotions frequently need approval. If yours are constantly getting knocked down, you will lose your effectiveness as a manager unless you learn to sell your ideas better. Frustrated employees may also take their problems to higher management. In most organizations people can take their complaints to the boss's boss or to the human resources department. This may put you on the defensive with higher management.

What about Complaints about Low Raises or No Raises at All?

Employees who have complaints about the amount and timing of their raises need immediate attention. Their upset can spread to other members of the staff and cause even bigger problems.

Certainly, if the performance appraisal meeting has already taken place by the time the salary action is approved and the manager is ready to speak to the employee about it, the employee should have a good idea of what's coming. If the employee's performance has been below standard, there should be no question about receiving a raise. If the person's work has met or exceeded expectations, he or she will legitimately expect a salary increase. If the employee expects a raise and doesn't get one or expects a bigger raise, the disappointment will show.

Very often people's expectations are unrealistic because they don't understand how salary decisions are made. If your compensation system is mysterious, your people will make wrong assumptions and may see the decisions as unfair. Tell them what the system is and how it works. If your system is kept a secret, most likely it isn't a fair one. Do what you can to change it. People who understand the system may still complain, but your explanations will be easier.

First of all, keep calm if the employee starts to blow off steam. Listen to the gripes, and think about whether they are legitimate and whether there is anything you can do about them. If they are well-founded complaints, perhaps you need to go to bat and see if you can't redress the grievance. Salary decisions are the time when it becomes apparent that first-line managers and supervisors have responsibility without authority. Most managers can recommend, but cannot make final, decisions about salary. This means we have to learn to sell our recommendations up the line. If we can get approvals for the increases we want to give our people, we can reward our high performers. Unfortunately this is not always the case. Some managers are more successful than others in developing these skills. If you are one whose recommendations fall on deaf ears, you may need to learn to be more convincing on those occasions. Then again, the management you work for may really be "deaf" to pleas for better salaries.

Some companies act as if the way to deal with salaries is to pay as little as possible. Salary expenses certainly need to be kept under control, but it is unrealistic to believe that employees will continue to perform at the highest levels without any real raises. After a while their most ambitious people will leave, and they will be left with people whose performance has deteriorated because of lack of reinforcement. Mediocre salaries attract and keep only mediocre people.

If an employee is disappointed with the size or frequency of salary increases, you may see that employee's performance diminish. Some people quit, but others stay, slow down, and start to do everything by the book. A good relationship between boss and subordinate may be easily ruined if the employee feels his or her efforts are going unrewarded. If corporations reward good performance with high raises, we have to face the fact that employees will then interpret low raises or no raises as punishment. In inflationary times, no raise or a low raise can mean, in effect, a cut in salary. All this is less of a problem if the employee is not one of your best. When low performers get mad and go away, it's one thing. But losing a good person, either to another firm or to low-level performance, is something to avoid. The most successful managers are often those who are best at dividing up the salary pie.

In making salary decisions, remember that you want the differences in levels of performance to show up in the differences in people's salaries. Also remember that some people need attention more often than others and that you may be better off giving your less secure people lower increases more often.

Sometimes there just isn't money for raises. When the company is doing poorly, you may not be able to give a raise even to your best people. In this case, you need to be honest about what is happening.

Say, "I wish I could give you a bigger raise, but I can't right now, even though ordinarily your performance would merit one." Reward the person in other ways—with praise certainly, but with time off or permission to attend conferences or conventions, or opportunities to attend training programs. Look for assignments that the person will find particularly rewarding. In other words, find rewards other than money that you can give the person. Of course, if the money issue becomes acute, you may have to face the fact that you will lose the person despite the other rewards.

You may have tried to get a better raise for the person and failed. If the problem is not one of profitability but just that your management turned you down, you may not want to tell the employee the truth. I think it's a mistake to say, "I tried to get you a bigger raise, but they turned me down." First of all, too many bosses use this as an excuse, often when it is not true. They don't want to take responsibility for their own decisions so they blame "upper management." Many employees are already aware of this ploy and won't believe it. Even if you have a gullible employee who would believe it and even if it is true, it's still not a good idea to say it. You would only be admitting that you are powerless to influence those above you on the employee's behalf. No one wants to work for such a boss.

What about the Person Who Expects a Promotion that Won't Come?

This is at least as difficult as the problem of the missing pay raise we've just discussed. And since it's no picnic to face an employee who feels passed over for a promotion, many managers avoid discussing promotions at all for fear of raising employee expectations. They feel the best way to keep this kind of disappointment under control is to keep expectations as low as possible. But avoiding the issue will not work.

Most employees feel they have the right to discuss their prospects for promotion with their bosses. Many of them have taken their jobs because they felt the position offered opportunities for advancement. We all know that you can't expect to attract the best people unless the job offers such opportunities. The person's future is often an easy topic for discussion when we are trying to get the best person for the job, but we may be reluctant to discuss that same future once the person accepts the job.

Advancement is a natural expectation in American businesses. Rightly or wrongly, our culture encourages people to expect to move up socially and economically. These expectations are practically in the air we breathe as kids. In a sense, everyone expects to advance. If employees receive highly complimentary performance reviews, they will naturally expect a promotion. Sometimes people don't think much about what that promotion will mean beyond higher pay and greater status, but they think they want it nonetheless.

Some people feel they want to advance, but really have no concrete ideas about what kind of higher level position they really want. This seems to me to be the greatest block to most people's advancement. Many people have the potential and can develop the needed skills, but they don't progress because they don't know what they want. I see this vague ambition often. Sometimes I think that the people who feel it really don't want more responsible jobs or are somehow psychologically unprepared to see themselves in these jobs. They seem to lack real drive.

Of course there are also people who know exactly what they want but are totally incapable of doing the work they think they can do. In an attempt to be kind or to encourage good performance in the current job, managers often encourage these false expectations. We need instead to help employees be realistic about their goals.

Above all, it is important for managers to know what their employees' expectations are. Not knowing could lead to wrong assumptions, disappointment, and loss of enthusiasm. What is most likely to happen is that the employee will expect more than he or she gets. When this is the case the manager must decide whether the employee's expectations are realistic.

I can't go on here without saying that judging people's potential is a difficult task and that gross errors are made. To find proof of this, all you need to do is think of all the people you know who have left one organization where they were dead-ended only to achieve great success in another organization where their potential was realized. Please take care with these decisions; they are important ones. Commercial over. Let's go on.

We must learn to avoid giving people unrealistic expectations. Here's how to do this.

Make Only Short-Term Plans

You are very limited in how much you can predict. Long-term plans are good to think about, but let the employee do the long-term speculation. You may even encourage long-term speculation, but don't engage in it. You have no real way of knowing what jobs will open when, how the employee's skill and motivation might develop, how the person's values might change, or how the economy or the environment might affect job possibilities.

Give the Employee
the Information to Make Judgments

Rather than guiding the person to your prediction, let the employee make the predictions. Even more important, let the employee decide what would be the best "future" to pursue. Whenever I hear managers trying to talk their employees into following a certain career path, I think of the character in the movie *The Graduate* who had only one word for Benjamin (Dustin Hoffman)—"plastics."

Don't Overstate
the Employee's Capabilities

In an effort to be encouraging and to generate enthusiasm, some managers will give employees a big buildup. It's fun because it makes employees happy, but it may have tragic results later on. People waste their time pursuing a career goal they will never achieve. They end up feeling like failures, and you end up the target of the frustration.

Never Say Anything
That Sounds Like a Promise

As a matter of fact, you should actively avoid being misinterpreted. Say, "I can't make any promises," or "These are only possibilities, and I want to make sure that you don't take what I am saying as a prediction or a promise."

Talk about More Than One Possibility

Talking about alternatives will do two things: It will keep what you say from sounding like a promise, and it will help the employee learn to keep options open.

You may also want to encourage your employee to get other opinions about possibilities for promotion. Career counselors in human resources departments often help people to answer such questions. You may also put your employee in touch with managers in other departments. As is true in other areas, getting many opinions may lead to better decisions. It will mean your prejudices will have less influence on the employee's choices.

A manager may encourage an employee's false expectations because she is reluctant to tell the employee the truth. Instead of saying, "I don't think you're qualified," she says, "I wish I could have given you the promotion, but it wasn't my decision." This is a temporary fix. What will the manager say the next time the subject comes up? And the subject will come up again since the employee has been led to believe there is hope.

If you are already faced with an employee who will not receive the promotion because he lacks the qualifications, there are only two steps you can take, and you must take them both. First tell the person the truth: tell him that he is not qualified and *why.* Say exactly what you think is missing. Then help the employee to develop the skills or knowledge needed to qualify or help the person to adopt more realistic goals.

Sometimes the problem is not the employee's qualifications but a paucity of opportunities in the organization. This sets up an entirely different set of dynamics.

Many times we have employees whose performance is high and who have potential to move up but for whom there are no higher level jobs available. Sometimes supervisors try to create higher level positions for these people, and sometimes they succeed. But many first-line supervisors and middle managers cannot do this. In large companies, new job descriptions have to be written, and job evaluation committees must approve such actions. (There are, of course, good reasons for this: Companies must protect themselves from abuses in this regard, and consistency in evaluating work is needed to comply with equal pay for equal work laws.) However, we may have an ambitious and capable employee who wants to get ahead. We fear losing the person if we have no promotion to offer. And sometimes we have none.

The incidence of this problem is likely to increase over the next several years as the baby-boom babies reach their middle years. The same crowd that caused schools to go on double sessions in the 1950s is now ready for management jobs. This glut of people in their thirties follows closely what amounted to a shortage of people in that age group because of low birthrates during the depression and World War II. This means that a decade ago there weren't enough people in their thirties to fill the middle management ranks. Industry had to reach to younger people to fill those jobs. It was a time of "fast-track" careers. For a while skyrocketing progress began to look like the norm. Then came the baby boom (and unfortunately, at the same time a period of slow, if any, growth for most industries), and the situation was reversed. There were many people and hardly any jobs. But today's ambitious young managers have observed the careers of their predecessors and expect not only to rise but to rise quickly. The result is a great deal of frustration.

In some instances we need to resign ourselves to losing some of our best people because we cannot offer them advancement. This is true especially in industries where growth is lowest. If you are in a low-growth or no-growth business, you can expect that most of the most ambitious people will leave and head for the places where there are greater opportunities. I think, however, that if slow growth continues, we will see a drop in the number of opportunities everywhere, and we will see less job-hopping. People will just know that there are no greener pastures. But this doesn't mean that they will settle in to work hard in stagnant jobs. Managers will have to look for ways outside the old high-raise/big-promotion cycle to keep these people enthusiastic. Here are some suggestions.

Discover and Analyze Each Person's Needs

As far as I can see, there aren't going to be stock answers for this problem. Basic needs for money and security will be met. If times are really bad, I guess people will be glad to have any kind of job. Nobody wants to see that happen. Beyond that, people will be seeking to satisfy other needs: for some it will be recognition or status, for others it will be flexibility so they can pursue other interests—spend more time with their families, travel, work on rewarding projects outside of work. Others will want opportunities to learn new skills. We are coming to a time where meshing the needs of the business with the needs of the workers will not be just a good idea. It may be critical to getting enthusiastic commitment from our people.

Allow Maximum Participation in Decisions

Let the employee help find ways to make the job more satisfying. Nobody knows better than the employee what will make the difference between a job that motivates and one that doesn't.

Delegate Whatever You Can

Instead of just allowing the person to participate in the decision-making process, give the employee all the authority and autonomy you can.

Use Job Enrichment

This doesn't mean that you just give people more to do; it does mean that you organize the work in ways that give people challenging and interesting jobs. It is more or less the opposite of the assembly line technique of fractionating jobs and making people interchangeable parts of the process. Job enrichment may mean reorganizing whole departments. We may have to do that to keep up or raise our employees' productivity.

Use Appraisal to Give Needed Recognition

The high levels of communication and interaction required by the performance planning and appraisal process are essential in this situation. The process will help ensure that people get the recognition they deserve. Although words of praise will not work forever, there is no point in not using them to the extent that they will.

Be as imaginative and flexible as you can in this. Work hard to break down the organization's resistance to innovative ways of treating people. Whatever else you do, if you are a manager, encouraging good performers is your job.

In the final analysis, you may have to let some of your best people go, either to other parts of the organization or even to other companies. If they are dead-ended, you have to expect that. You may even have to encourage it rather than see them stagnate and their performance deteriorate.

Using the Appraisal Process with Union Workers

Performance appraisal hasn't had a good reputation among workers. Probably because it has been based on the subjective opinion of supervisors and because it has been so widely abused, workers prefer that decisions about pay and status be based on a totally objective criterion —seniority. This is not to say that we cannot plan and appraise the work of union members. It merely means that the dynamics of the process will be very different, since administrative decisions will not be based on the results of the appraisal.

This is not necessarily bad. As a matter of fact, we have already said that the primary purpose of the planning and appraisal process should be to control work. If the appraisal process is used to make decisions about raises, promotions, and firings, these decisions should be made and discussed after the appraisal is completed. Where union contracts dictate raises and seniority is used for other administrative decisions, the planning and appraisal process can still be carried out for its primary purpose.

The major difficulty with performance planning in this setting is that many union-represented hourly workers have jobs that are fractionated, boring, repetitive, and basically unsatisfying. Therefore it would be hard to think of planning such work and setting standards beyond the routine so many a day or such and such a reject rate. There is, of course, the possibility of performance improvement and personal growth goals. If your people are unionized but do work that lends itself to planning, then you should certainly make a thorough work plan with each employee. Even if the work is assembly line in nature, you can still plan parts of it. Using the planning and appraisal cycle to keep the lines of communication open can save you headaches, especially in a union shop.

Union officials tell me the most frequent difficulty with disciplinary action arises because a supervisor's warning has been vague. Employees then don't realize that dismissal is impending. Of course it is possible that employees understand, but say they don't. In any event, this just points up the need to be clear and specific and to put things in writing.

Union employees also have the right to have a union representative at any meeting that they suspect may result in disciplinary action. Since appraisal meetings fall into this category, you must allow the union representative to come to the meeting. (Boss-subordinate relations are at a sorry pass if an employee feels the need to have a third party present for performance appraisal.)

When firing an employee looks inevitable, one technique that helps some managers is this: If you have tried to bring the person's performance around on your own and nothing has worked, consider going to the union with the problem. Say, "I don't want to fire Joan, but . . ." We talk a lot about how the adversary relationship between union and management is bad, but perhaps we can begin to cooperate at the most basic levels. Contrary to popular belief, most unions do not want to protect the jobs of proven shirkers. You may get some support and help by looking for cooperation instead of assuming you'd only get roadblocks.

Appraising Executives

Just as it does with workers on the line, appraising the people at the other end of the organization chart presents special difficulties. Many organizations will implement performance appraisal systems from the bottom up. They will begin with a system for appraising nonexempt positions, then professional, technical, and middle management people, and last, if ever, the executives. This way the people whose work is ostensibly the most critical (Isn't that why they get paid more?) are the last ones to get appraised.

There are several excuses for this upside-down approach. For one thing, top executives often feel that it is inappropriate for them to be appraised. The typical reasons given for this are all true. Executive jobs are often one of a kind in the organization. More important, executive work requires complex skills of judgment and decision making. A top manager may be involved in 30 or more activities in one day. These activities are difficult to categorize and judge especially in the short range. For this reason most executive appraisal systems are aimed at measuring outcomes. The managers are measured on whether they achieve agreed-upon goals. This seems fair, but with top executive work, appraisal by objectives can cause problems. I am not suggesting that objectives should not be set. They should be. But the problem is one of timing. Most appraisal systems are, at their longest, an annual cycle. This means that the outcomes on which the executive will be appraised have to be evident within a year. This causes executives to emphasize short-range planning and short-range results and may lead to mortgaging the future for good results or a good bonus this year.

Much of the work executives should be doing has only ambiguous results over the short haul. To look good at appraisal time executives have to milk today's good ideas and often kill what may be tomorrow's for the sake of a good bottom line. Of course, our system emphasizes short-term profitability in other ways as well. Quarterly earnings and annual dividends are seen as the important measures of the health of a business. Executives are rewarded or punished (fired or shunted into unimportant jobs) based on these short-term measures. But they are seldom rewarded or punished for their long-term successes or failures. The failures are especially worrisome since they can adversely affect so many people. Top executives decide to market certain products or to make certain capital investments that are sometimes predictably dumb ideas, and five years later when the products aren't selling or the investments aren't paying off, they are busy collecting a quarter of a million dollars a year in retirement benefits. Perhaps what we need is a system for rewarding executives after their ideas have proved to be good ones. Perhaps we need a system that takes into account decisions made three to five years ago and tries to evaluate plans for the future.

Appraising Group Efforts

If you want a new bathroom built in your house, you may need as many as seven people: a plumber, a carpenter, an electrician, a tile setter, a taper and spackler, a painter, and a wallpaper hanger. When we had a crowd like that working in our house, I noticed right away that although each of them was skilled in a specialty, none of them had the least notion that they were working together to build a bathroom. More than likely, they got in one another's way. It's like that with much of what should be group work. In Chapter 3, we talked about planning a group's work with the group, where there is one goal, making one plan. Follow-up and appraisal then should be done the same way.

Performance appraisal systems usually ignore the dynamics of the group. We may say we value teamwork, but the way we do appraisals hardly ever fosters it. Sometimes in college courses group work is set up, and then the members of the group all get the same mark. This doesn't happen much in business, and perhaps it should. If everyone knows ahead of time that all the members of the group will receive the same appraisal, the group members will feel more compelled to cooperate and make it work. (In sports this works very well. You either win the World Series or you don't—as a team.)

There are many instances in which group cooperation can make or break a project. In such situations, we can use artificial methods of fostering group cooperation: by rating each person on how well he or she cooperates with others. Although that would encourage team identification, we might ensure it if everyone knew that each person on the team would receive the same performance rating.

Some observers see trends in this direction. As we move from an industrial to a service and information-based society, team performance will become increasingly important. It is becoming less possible to isolate one person's contribution. It may, as we have said, even become counterproductive to try. We have been fostering competition among our employees by rating them individually (and even in some companies by saying that only such and such a percentage can get the highest rating). Now we need systems that will reward cooperation instead of pitting employees against one another.

If you manage people whose contributions are largely interdependent, begin by planning the major part of the work at the group level. (Performance improvement and personal growth goals can still be set individually.) Periodically review progress and solve problems at staff meetings, and then hold the appraisal meeting with the whole group. This meeting will require a great deal of skill. You will have to keep the group on track, make sure they concentrate on assessing how the group performed, and keep them from evaluating one another's characters. If you are going to try such an approach, you may want to start by having a consultant to support your efforts until the group gets used to the new system.

Summary

- Problems of organization and structure must be solved before performance planning and appraisal can succeed.
- Managers whose style is threatening or whose technical knowledge is totally lacking will not be able to plan and appraise productively.
- If your people know a lot more about the work than you do:
  - Admit that there's a gap.
  - Express respect for the employees' knowledge.
  - Say what you can contribute.
  - But don't apologize for being a manager.
- Always allow the employee to read your written appraisal.
- If the employee thinks the appraisal isn't fair:
  - Listen to the complaint; avoid defensiveness.
  - Follow any formal grievance procedure dictated by policy.
  - Allow the employee to talk it over with your boss or someone from personnel.
  - Let the employee write a "dissenting" opinion for the file.
- In appraising older workers:
  - Never base any decisions about an employee on age; it's illegal.
  - Plan as you would with any other employee.
  - If you are younger or less experienced, avoid defensiveness by expressing your respect for the employee's capabilities.
  - Don't raise the issue of age. If you need to know the employee's plans, just ask about plans.
  - Help ease the employee's transition to the role of mentor and conservator by valuing this work and rewarding the person for it.
  - Discuss benefit changes when the employee nears age 65.
- For the self-motivated superstar:
  - Be generous with tangible and intangible rewards.
  - Find out why the person works so hard, and try to keep meeting those needs on the job.

- Keep the person growing with challenging assignments.
- Be careful not to raise unrealistic expectations for raises or promotions.
  - Be specific about rewards.
  - Don't make promises that require another person's approval.
  - Make only short-term plans.
  - Give the employee information to make realistic judgments.
  - Don't overstate the employee's capabilities.
  - Talk about options.
- To deal with an employee who expects a higher raise:
  - Let the employee blow off steam.
  - Intercede for the person with a legitimate complaint.
  - For some people, higher raises at long intervals are best; for others, smaller ones at shorter intervals work better. Be sure your timing is as good as you can make it.
  - If the problem is a lack of funds, try to find other ways to reward good performance.
- If you have no promotion to give, and one is expected or deserved:
  - Be willing to discuss realistic expectations.
  - Again, be careful of making vague promises.
  - Tell the person the truth if he or she isn't qualified for the next level.
  - Help the person to develop the needed qualifications or to adopt realistic goals.
  - If there are no opportunities in your area, try to create some. If you can't, be aware that the person may leave.
- To try to keep up the motivation of those whose careers are stalled:
  - Discover and analyze each person's needs.
  - Allow maximum participation in decisions.
  - Delegate whatever you can.
  - Use job enrichment.
- With union employees:
  - Allow the person to bring a union representative to any meeting that concerns performance appraisal.
  - Consider involving the union in your efforts to improve an individual's performance.
- The unstructured nature of executive work makes these jobs difficult to plan and appraise. Most executive appraisal systems, therefore, concentrate on results.
- Where group efforts are critical:
  - Plan, follow up, and appraise the group.
  - Where overall ratings are necessary, consider giving all members of the group the same rating.

Chapter 9

Corporate Systems: How They Fit In

Until now we have been talking about the right way to do performance planning and appraisal and ignoring the fact that if you work for a large corporation you probably have a form you must fill out and a system you must follow. Now let's deal with how you can do the job of managing in the productive way we have described *and* meet the requirements of your company's system. First let's review the kinds of systems.

Some of the systems include a performance planning element, many do not. The first two systems do, and they are very similar to the techniques you have been reading about thus far.

MBO

Many systems have been invented to make performance planning a part of performance appraisal. The best known of these is management by objectives (MBO). As a matter of fact, MBO has become the most widely used form of performance planning, especially for managerial work.

The system itself is a model of logic and simplicity. The results an employee must achieve are decided upon, sometimes by the manager alone, more often by the manager and the employee working together. These goals must be specific and measurable and are connected with a time schedule. They may include regular work objectives—projects or activities the employee is normally involved in—or they may be problem-solving objectives or personnel growth objectives—where the employee and manager agree that the employee will concentrate on overcoming some performance deficiency or developing some new skill. These objectives become the measures of the employee's performance. Evaluation is then based on whether the employee met the objectives within the time period.

This system gives the manager a great deal of flexibility in choosing priorities and setting standards. It also allows for the employee participation that we have said is so desirable. The MBO approach has many other advantages. By setting up a plan at the outset against which the employee's performance will later be measured, MBO takes the focus off the employee's personality and places it where it belongs—on what the employee did or didn't do. This means that employees can more readily accept the results. MBO concentrates on the individual and doesn't lump all employees of the same job title into one category. It can also be easily meshed with other business planning techniques. For instance, once a strategic plan is made, the goals can be broken down into individual objectives for employees. This takes performance planning and appraisal out of the realm of a "nice to have" personnel program and makes it an integral part of the management of an organization's business.

Since evaluating past objectives and setting new ones are done at the same time, MBO gives the manager a chance to focus on the future rather than the past. This can decrease an employee's defensiveness if the manager has to discuss performance shortcomings. In this way the MBO system casts the manager in the role of coach and helper, whereas traditional performance appraisal makes the manager a judge or critic. The MBO system is also adaptable to all levels within an organization, from executives to workers on the line.

Like all systems, MBO does have some drawbacks. For one, although it is most useful in ensuring or improving employee performance and meeting employee development needs, it is not the neatest way to figure out who should get how much in a raise, nor is it useful in gathering data for personnel plans. MBO produces descriptive narratives rather than easily manipulated numbers that can be used for test validation or salary administration. One of the biggest problems with MBO is that sometimes an objective belonging to one employee requires the cooperation and support of others. It is difficult to set specific goals and establish objective standards in such cases. Say Harry doesn't get the manuals out on time because the print shop was backlogged and couldn't do the work within their normal time frame. Do we blame the print shop or do we say Harry missed his goal because he should have allowed for some very unlikely delays?

The MBO system also requires that managers develop certain skills: job analysis skills so they can break jobs down into activities that can be stated as objectives, communication skills so they can reach agreement with employees on what is expected, organization skills so they can keep track of the follow-up work they must do. And MBO requires time, at least two meetings with each employee in any planning period.

The rewards of using this system seem to be worth the trouble though since so many major corporations have adopted the technique. Research confirms this: Instituting MBO systems has consistently led to improvements in employee performance.

Management Contracts

Some organizations use what are called "management contracts" to accomplish the job of performance planning and appraisal. In this approach the manager negotiates a performance "contract" with the employee. The contract, like the objectives in an MBO system, must be specific, measurable, and time-based. But the contract also contains the standards by which the employee's performance will be judged. Sometimes it also states the rewards the employee will receive. Then the judging seems eminently fair.

Sister Mary Catharine O'Connor, to whom this book is dedicated, gave me my first example of the fairness of this approach. In her English literature courses she would begin each semester by handing out a sheet of paper with a line across the middle. If you wanted a C in the course, you had to do all the things listed at the top of the page. If you wanted a B, you had to do all the things listed at the top and one of those listed at the bottom. For an A you did everything at the top, plus two of the things at the bottom. The hard and fast rule was that everything at the top was basic. No matter what else you did, you couldn't get even a C unless you completed those assignments. After years of being judged by various teachers' subjective systems, we were slow to catch on. But what a relief it was once we did. No more high academic scores for having the right personality traits. What was expected was made clear from the beginning, and nothing mattered except whether you did the work. Everyone agreed that Sister Mary Catharine's courses were tough, but no one complained that she wasn't fair.

In an effort to achieve this kind of fairness, the management contract method of planning seeks to define very carefully beforehand how an employee will be judged. Then there are no surprises at "report card" time.

Job Descriptions

Some companies use job descriptions to communicate expectations and to judge an employee's work. These may be useful as jumping-off points and may even be sufficient for some simple straightforward jobs. Of course, job descriptions have a number of other uses: Most companies use them to set salary grades and ranges; they can be given to prospective employees so they will understand more about the job they are applying for. However, they are not always useful as the sole basis for communicating expectations or judging performance.

The first difficulty arises from the way most job descriptions are prepared. They are usually written by a manager, sometimes with the help of compensation people in the personnel department, but usually without the participation of the employee. This lack of employee participation can cause problems in understanding and acceptance. Sometimes incumbent employees find that the job their boss and the staff from personnel have described doesn't seem to be the job they have been doing.

There are worse problems with using job descriptions on their own. They are usually written to cover several jobs that are similar but not exactly the same. When this is the case, they become general and vague, two qualities notably dangerous when one is trying to communicate work expectations to an employee. Similarly, these descriptions usually have setting salary levels as their primary purpose. Words are chosen not because they will clearly communicate to the employee what is expected, but because they will convince the salary committee to give the job a certain rating or to put it in a certain category with other jobs. All this makes the document useful only as a beginning step in setting up a performance plan.

If we take the job description as a basis, we can link it with specific descriptions of work the employee must do and specific standards of performance—descriptions of how we expect the finished "product" to look. For instance, if René's job description says:

Contribute data for the annual financial plan.

The supplement to it might say:

- Gather sales data for each item in the Parachute Luggage line by month and region.
- Analyze data for the past 24 months and identify trends.
- Project sales by month and region for the next 12 months.
- Submit a report of your analysis with data tables attached by the second Monday in September.

You can see that the objective here is to take the vague generalities of the job description and turn them into clear explanations of what is wanted. Then there can be no question in the employee's mind about what to do. The work will be more likely to meet the corporation's needs, and there will be no difficulty discussing the issue later. You can do this. Better yet, your employee should do it. The employee may know more and may welcome the opportunity to show off some knowledge.

If the manager in our example were to try to base a later appraisal on the job description statement alone, I can foresee the following: René guesses at what information is needed for the annual financial plan, does some unnecessary as well as some necessary work, tries very hard, but falls far short of the mark. Imagine the conversation that might ensue between her and her manager, the claims and counter-claims about whether the responsibility as outlined on the job description has been fulfilled. That conversation seems worth avoiding. Of course, the real payoff of specificity is productivity; our employees give us what we need and on time, and they don't waste effort on unnecessary work.

BARS

BARS stands for behaviorally anchored rating scales. This method attempts to combine trait rating with the specificity needed for fair and useful performance appraisal. Rather than using global terms like "gets along well with others" or "attitude," the BARS method uses careful job analysis to determine what behaviors are actually required in a certain job. The required behavior patterns become "anchors" for a rating scale.

For example, an old-fashioned trait-rating scale might have a category called "customer contact" and give a manager a scale of 1 to 5 on which to rate an employee's performance in this category. A BARS form might have several behaviors listed for this category. One might look like this:

5	4	3	2	1
Always greets customers			Ignores customers	
and asks if he/she may			unless they demand	
be of help			attention	

Clearly this gives more specific information, but also requires more work to develop. The procedure for developing a BARS form has five steps:

1. *Critical incidents* are developed. People who know the job well describe specific examples of effective and ineffective behaviors.
2. *Performance dimensions* are developed. The behaviors are grouped into categories, usually by the same people who came up with them in the first place.
3. The descriptions are *retranslated.* That is, another group repeats step 2, deciding which behavior fits into which category.
4. In *scaling,* the second group decides what kind of a scale to use for rating each description of effective and ineffective behavior. The resulting behavioral scales may be statistically tested so that only valid measures are included in the final form.
5. The BARS form is developed from those items that pass the tests developed in step 4.

The process is complex, but it can produce a rating form that is based on relevant and specific measures of performance. Since the BARS method uses a scale, it produces data useful for salary decisions and other administrative uses. It is also relatively easy to use from a manager's point of view and requires less training and explanation when it is implemented. Because the measures of performance result from a careful analysis of the requirements of the job, BARS produces clear definitions and a set of criteria that are easily observable. This makes it relatively simple for a manager to evaluate a person's performance. Also, because they are job related, the evaluations are considered easier to defend if legal problems arise.

There are, of course, some drawbacks. The most obvious is the cost of developing a BARS form. Each one requires the careful and systematic work of two groups of people, an expert who can coordinate the work, and probably some statistical analysis. BARS do make it easier for the manager, but he or she is still required to make judgments and careful observations of employees. Supervisors or managers may have difficulty matching things the employee does with what is listed and categorized on the form. A BARS form also does not provide any vehicle for planning the work to be done.

BARS are most useful where ratings are needed and less useful where performance feedback is critical. They can be used as year-end evaluation tools in systems that also employ performance planning methods. I can't imagine BARS being used alone in managerial jobs. Perhaps because the concept is new or perhaps because its use is limited to first-line supervisory jobs and below, BARS has not been widely used.

Hybrid Systems

Each of the planning systems I've described is more useful for some of the ends of performance appraisal than others. In an attempt to develop a system that will satisfy all needs, some companies have looked for ways to measure both outcome and behavior. These systems often combine a planning system, like MBO, and rating systems, like BARS. These combinations, sometimes called hybrid systems, try to take advantage of the strengths and avoid the weaknesses of only one approach. By coming at the problem from two angles, combination systems can serve the employee's and manager's needs for a method of planning and feedback and the organization's need for ratings that can be used for administrative purposes—salary administration, test validation, and the like. For organizations that want to cover all the bases, hybrid systems can work. However, we need to be careful about going too far too fast. In organizations where no formal performance appraisal systems have been used, a complicated hybrid system may be too much all at once. You as a manager would be better off starting out with a straightforward planning and feedback system like the one this book advocates and then going on to expand the system once it is working well.

Subjective Systems

Despite the fact that there are so many better ideas around these days, many companies still use systems and forms that require supervisors to make subjective judgments about their subordinates. If you work for such a company, you probably think that what we have said is all well and good, but you probably still have to fill out the inadequate form because it is required by the personnel department. Well, I'm not here to tell you to defy the edicts of your personnel department, but I am saying that certain forms will interfere with, rather than aid, performance appraisal. These forms fall into four categories:

Global Ratings

Some forms merely ask the manager to give an overall rating of the employee and perhaps to explain the rating. No performance dimensions are given, just a numerical scale, or a list of terms—for example, outstanding, above average, average, fair, poor.

Essay Format

Some "forms" are not a form at all but just a request that managers write whatever they feel is important about the employee in a memo and send the memo to be put in the personnel file and used as justification for administrative decisions.

Ranking Form

Used most widely in the military, this form asks the manager to rank employees either in relation to each other—Ann is best, Neil is next, and so on—or in categories—top 1 percent, top 5 percent, top 30 percent, and so forth. Again, these ratings are not typically based on defined, job-related measures of performance.

Trait-Rating Scales

This is the most prevalent of the subjective forms. The form usually lists traits like initiative, dependability, and judgment (which we criticized in Chapter 2). Across the top there is either a rating scale of numbers or those familiar words.

There are several problems with these subjective approaches, not the least of which is that if they are ever used in court, they will probably not hold up. Judges frown upon systems that are not based on specific, job-related criteria. These forms are all vague. Aside from the possible legal problems, they are not really useful. They make the appraisal interview extremely awkward as anyone who has had to discuss "attitude" with an employee will attest.

They are also highly susceptible to error. The vague terms mean different things to different managers, and since there are no constraints, the manager's errors of judgment may go undetected. The errors may go undetected, but the appraisal form itself may get lots of attention. It is filed and may haunt the employee forever.

Managers often protest that the traits listed on their forms are really important. They say, "But I want my employees to be cooperative." I say fine, but you need to define what "cooperative" means in specific, job-related terms. In fact, that is the key to using the form you are required to use and still doing the productive and legal thing.

One of the more serious problems with these subjective systems is that they play into the manager's tendency to think of performance problems as personality issues. Then the appraisal interview becomes controlled by the form rather than by the manager.

Dealing with the Form

Give the Employee a Blank Form at the Outset Do this when you are preparing the employee for the planning meeting. Explain to the employee that the form is one required by the personnel department. *Don't* bad-mouth the form or the personnel department. Just say that you want to use some of the time at the planning meeting to relate the work plan to the items on the form.

Use the Work Plan to "Define" the Traits Match the items on the work plan with traits on the form. If one of the traits is "judgment" and an item on the work plan is "analyze the department's supply needs and recommend cost cuts," you can say that finding ways of cutting costs without sacrificing efficiency would be considered a demonstration of good judgment.

List Examples of Behavior Illustrating the Traits If some of the items on the form don't match with work goals, write a list of behaviors required in the job that you feel would constitute high performance for each trait. For instance, under "cooperative" you might list: "pitches in to help fellow employees when they are overloaded and he or she has the time."

Consider Involving the Employee in Completing the Form After the final appraisal discussion is over, some managers fill out the form with the employee. If you do this, you can discuss how you are making each judgment and why. The final answers must reflect your ideas, but involving the employee and discussing it can prevent misunderstandings later. Some managers just give the form to the employee and say, "You fill it out and I'll sign it." That's a cop-out. And it makes the employee think you don't care. Don't do it.

Prevent a "Good" System from Failing

I've never heard of a perfect performance appraisal system. Even the best designed ones are subject to abuse and elicit complaints from the managers who have to use them. I sympathize with managers who are trying to do a good job and run up against problems with cumbersome or counterproductive systems. But managers are the ones who most easily misuse the performance appraisal system. There are many ways to do this.

Managers, like anyone else, may be bigots. Bigoted people probably shouldn't be managers at all, but when they are, their prejudices may show up on the performance appraisal form. They find "logical" reasons for giving low ratings to minorities, women, older workers, or whatever group they dislike. As a matter of fact, unscrupulous managers may use performance appraisal forms to make their bigotry look respectable.

Some managers are angry about the appraisals they have received from their own bosses. They find it impossible to express that anger directly at the person who offended them, so they turn around and give a low rating to their subordinates. A manager who misuses performance appraisal in this way might be thinking, "If my boss thinks I'm average, the people who work for me must be even lower."

Some managers, of course, simply ignore the form. They don't fill it out and send it in. There are variations on this theme. Some fill it out and send it in but never talk to the employee about it. Some fill it out, discuss it, and send it in, but they never really appraise the employee's performance. They just make sure to say mostly positive things. That way there is no pain involved for the manager or the employee, and everyone is "satisfied." Some, as we have said, just give the form to the employee and say, "Here, you fill this out, and I'll sign it and send it in."

Avoidance in one way or another is probably the most common abuse of performance appraisal. It is understandable. People don't like to tell other people that they are average or worse. As long as managers and employees see the appraisal as an appraisal of the person rather than the work, both will seek to avoid it (even though the manager knows it's necessary, and the employee genuinely wants feedback on performance). Both still fear rejection. The employee worries about feeling rejected because of a low rating. The manager fears being rejected by the employee who is disappointed or angered by a low rating.

Sometimes to avoid the problems of communicating with the employee about upsetting things managers cheat: They fill out two forms, one positive and one negative. They then show the complimentary one to the employee, but send the other one to the personnel department.

Some managers are reluctant to discuss performance appraisal because they are reluctant to share any information with their employees. They feel information is power and the best way to preserve and increase their own power is to communicate as little as possible. For some, this prejudice against communicating extends to their subordinates, but not to their peers or superiors. These managers see interacting with peers and superiors as a way of increasing their status in the organization. They don't want to be identified too closely with those at a lower level so they spend as little time with them as possible. If you don't believe this, just think of how differently you react when you hear that someone is in a meeting with the division president as opposed to a meeting with an assistant.

When we talked about assessing performance, we discussed the tendency of managers to rate everyone as high or average or low. These errors, well known to statisticians, make performance appraisal inaccurate and contribute to its unpopularity.

One of the subtler problems with these issues is that managers are often unaware of how they are behaving or why. They make errors in judgment, avoid communicating with their subordinates and believe that they are not doing these things. Their blind spots make these managers difficult to reach and train, even when others in the organization have recognized the problem.

Managers are certainly not the only ones who contribute to the failure of performance appraisal systems. Organizations create their own sets of problems.

Sometimes organizations make the basic error of not having a clear policy about performance appraisal and how it is to be carried out. Some organizations have a policy, but it is too extensive. The performance appraisal system is expected to do too many things, sometimes even conflicting things. Like any other system, performance appraisal can be ruined by unrealistic expectations.

Some organizations try to eliminate the management abuses we have discussed by having a good basic system, but then they strangle the system with too many controls. Managers have no flexibility in carrying out their responsibility. For instance, in many companies managers feel straitjacketed by the forced distribution rule—the requirement that managers rate only 10 percent of their employees in the highest rating and 20 percent in the next highest, and so on. A manager of one of America's most prestigious corporations once told me, "This is one of the heaviest crosses that management in my outfit has to bear."

The difficulty is that rules like forced distribution in effect set up competition among employees, when managers are trying to foster cooperation. Employees know that only a few can reach the highest ratings. This can cause the more desperate ones to resort to making the other person look bad so they can "score the highest." If your company has such a rule, I advise making the strongest case you can against it. It forces us as managers to tell the majority of our people they are less than wonderful when study results show people work best when they feel like winners. At the very least, minimize your discussion of this rule when discussing performance appraisal with your employees. Stick to the plan as the yardstick for how well they have done. Don't compare them to one another.

The problem is, of course, that the rule is there to keep managers from giving everyone the highest rating so they can give everyone the highest raise. As we have said, tying performance planning and appraisal too closely with salary action causes problems. In attempting to eliminate those problems, system designers add rules that further complicate the issue.

In some organizations, higher management may second-guess the immediate supervisor. Ratings or even statements may be changed by the boss before they are submitted to the personnel department. Sometimes managers force their subordinate managers to share these doctored appraisals with their employees. The supervisors are put in the difficult position of having to communicate with conviction opinions they don't hold. These poor people need acting lessons, not management training.

In many organizations this second-guessing applies to salary and promotion decisions. Managers are told they must appraise their employees, fill out forms, and make recommendations about job actions, but their recommendations are seldom carried out. The managers become frustrated and feel that the appraisal system isn't worth the work they have to put into it.

Few organizations properly train their managers to do performance planning and appraisal. The managers are just expected to do a complicated and critical job with little or no preparation. This lack of preparation leads to inconsistencies and failures. The vicious cycle of bad performance appraisal experiences leading to worse ones often causes organizations to conclude that what they need is a new system. Consultants are called in, new systems are invented and implemented with the same inattention to training. Here we go again.

Doing performance planning and appraisal is an essential part of a manager's job. As I have said before, I don't consider it another management task, but a method for managing. Certainly organizations will want to have systems to ensure that such important work gets done with some degree of consistency. If your organization needs to overhaul or reinvent its performance appraisal system, there are many things to think about. This is not a book about how to create a performance appraisal system for an organization, but if that is what you are going to do, consider these techniques:

Involve the Managers in the Design

The people who will be responsible for carrying out the policy should be involved in designing it. This will make it more practical and more palatable to them.

Involve the Employee Too

This will help you come up with a system that really meets the needs of the employees, and employees are more likely to view the system as fair if they have had a hand in designing it.

Design Some Flexibility into the System

Rigidity is a big problem with performance appraisal systems. It can lead to bureaucratic silliness such as managers having to appraise people who have just joined their staff, people they hardly know. To the extent that rigidity makes your new policy look foolish, it will fail. Unworkable policies get ridiculed and are finally ignored. Don't write a policy that will convince your managers that they work in the cuckoo's nest.

Get Top Management to Introduce It

The new system must be introduced as a management system. It should come from the highest level in the organization and not look like just another new form from the personnel department.

Make Training a Major Step
in the Implementation

Widespread and careful training of the managers who will operate the system will help ensure its success. This means including training in all the skills they need to do it well. You wouldn't think of implementing a new computer system without training the people who will operate it. Don't do this with a planning and appraisal system either. Your people are more important than your machines.

No performance planning and appraisal system can be foolproof. It is unrealistic to expect that anything so complex will be error-free, but it makes good business sense to create the best one we can. It may also keep you out of court, as we will see in the next chapter.

Summary

- Most corporations use one of the following systems for performance appraisal:
  - MBO
  - Management contracts
  - Job description
  - BARS
  - Hybrid systems
  - Global ratings
  - Essay format
  - Ranking form
  - Trait-rating scales
- If you use the job description, you and your employee may have to supplement vague, general statements with specific descriptions about what is required.

- How to handle a subjective performance appraisal form:
  - Give the employee a blank form at the outset.
  - Use the work plan to define the traits listed on the form or define the traits in terms of behavior.
- Consider involving the employee in completing the form, but don't hand it over totally to the employee.
- Performance appraisal is subject to many abuses:
  - Bigoted managers can use it against groups they dislike.
  - Some managers who get bad appraisals take this out on their employees.
  - Some managers avoid it by not filling out the form, by not discussing it, or by making it artificially positive to avoid confrontation.
  - A few managers will fill out two forms: a positive one to show the employee and a negative one for the file.
  - Some managers will be stingy with performance feedback because they feel information is power, and they don't want to give any power away.
  - Some managers are so busy scoring points with those above them that they have no time for their subordinates.
- Organizations can make performance appraisal difficult by:
  - Not having a clear policy
  - Having a system that is too complex
  - Overburdening the system by expecting it to do too much
  - Making it so controlled it is a straitjacket instead of a useful tool
  - Allowing higher levels of management to change what the immediate supervisor said
  - Not giving managers proper training
- Techniques that will help you invent a workable corporate system:
  - Involve the managers in the design.
  - Involve the employees too.
  - Design some flexibility into the system.
  - Make it a management program.
  - Train managers thoroughly in how to do it.
- There is no such thing as a foolproof performance appraisal system.

Chapter 10

Performance Appraisal and the Law

Because performance appraisal has been based largely on subjective ratings and personality traits, not job-related criteria, over the past ten years appraisals have increasingly become the target of federal regulation. Since appraisals are often used to make decisions about promotions and transfers, they are considered a test and are subject to the Equal Employment Opportunity Commission (EEOC) guidelines.

Many organizations have realized that accurate performance appraisal data is critical to their EEOC compliance efforts. They want to make sure that they are really promoting the best qualified candidates and that they will not wind up in court having to defend indefensible, subjective, or inaccurate appraisals. Although they are slightly more flexible with appraisals than they are with out-and-out employment exams, the courts still expect appraisals used for decision making to be fair. Managers who are going to protect themselves and their companies need to know the law and how to keep performance appraisal productive *and* legal.

To begin with, let's summarize how the law and performance appraisal interrelate. Basically, the law requires that performance appraisal be:

- Job-related and valid
- Based on a thorough job analysis
- Standardized for all employees
- Not biased against any race, color, sex, religion, or nationality
- Not based on subjective or vague criteria
- Performed by people who have adequate knowledge of the person and the job

The Essential Issue Is Validity

The law requires that performance appraisal systems be valid, and validity may have several meanings. Basically a performance appraisal system is valid if the company using it can demonstrate that the system accurately measures job-related performance criteria. We can prove validity by testing a system using established statistical testing techniques or by establishing what is called content validity. This means that we can show we judge our employees on what the job requires, the whole job and nothing but the job. A legal performance appraisal system also makes sure that the emphasis given any job-related criterion is appropriate—that we don't disportionately emphasize any particular job requirement.

Most companies do not try to validate their appraisal systems statistically. They rely on content validity; others tempt fate by having systems that are subjective and impossible to defend. Traditional graphic, trait-rating forms, for instance, typically ask supervisors to rate employees on such nebulous criteria as "gets along well with others." These criteria are unlikely to hold up in court. BARS, on the other hand, are based on carefully established, statistically validated criteria and would very likely be legally defensible. Work-planning procedures, such as the process recommended in this book, have never been directly challenged in court. However, since they establish job-related criteria, they are considered to have content validity.

Just What Laws Apply

Mostly it is the EEOC laws that apply to performance appraisal. In case you haven't seen them a thousand times already, here they are:

The Equal Pay Act of 1963

This law says equal pay must be given for equal work. It impinges on the planning aspects of our system.

Title VII of the Civil Rights Act of 1964

Amended in 1972 and in 1978, this law prohibits employers from discriminating on the basis of sex, religion, race, color, or national origin. If an employee claims to have been discriminated against, the employer must prove that job-related criteria were used in making any judgments.

The Age Discrimination in Employment Act of 1967

This law, which was amended in 1974 and 1978, protects job applicants and employees aged 40 to 70 from discrimination. The upper limit of 70 does not apply to federal employees and soon may be removed for other employees as well.

The Vietnam Era Veterans Readjustment Assistantance Act of 1972

Since it was reenacted in 1974, this law has been known as the Vietnam Era Veterans Readjustment Act. It requires companies to take affirmative action in employing and promoting disabled veterans and veterans of the Vietnam war. This law was amended in 1976 and 1978 and applies to companies with $10,000 or more in government contracts.

The Rehabilitation Act of 1973

This law was also amended in 1974 and in 1978. It requires companies to take reasonable steps to accommodate the mental and physical needs of handicapped applicants and employees. The law applies only to the companies that have $2500 or more in government contracts.

The Privacy Act of 1974

This law protects the privacy of records that contain information about employees. It makes specific provision for medical and arrest records and other information that is ordinarily kept in personnel files. It also gives past and present employees of the federal government the right of access to their employment records. Several states, for example, California, Illinois, Massachusetts, New York, and Maine, have privacy acts that give employees certain rights regarding their personnel files. You need to become aware of what rules apply in your state.

Some Famous Cases

Several cases have tested the interpretation of these laws and given us precedents. Here are a few:

Brito v. Zia Company

This case concerned performance ratings used in layoffs. The court found that the supervisor's ratings were vague and subjective, that the ratings were made by supervisors who did not have sufficient contact with the employee to be able to reasonably judge performance, and that the appraisal forms were not administered under appropriately controlled conditions.

Albemarle Paper Co. v. Moody

This case involved discrimination in employment testing. Again the court found that the supervisor's appraisals were based on vague, subjective standards that were questionable in terms of job relatedness.

Griggs v. Duke Power Co.

The court opinion was that "Practices, procedures or tests, neutral on their face and even neutral in terms of intent, cannot be maintained if they operate to 'freeze' the status quo of prior discriminatory practices."

Rowe v. General Motors

In this race discrimination case, the court ruled that an all-white management may not be able to fairly evaluate the work of black and minority work forces unless they have a valid appraisal system and adequate training. Companies whose managers are all white, middle-aged males may need to prove that their performance appraisals are not indirectly contributing to discrimination against minorities, women, or workers over 40.

NLRB v. Weingarten, Inc.

In this case brought by the National Labor Relations Board, the court ruled that any employee who suspects that a meeting may lead to disciplinary action has the right to ask for union representation at the meeting. Any performance appraisal meeting, I would think, falls into this category.

EEOC Guidelines

The Equal Employment Opportunity Commission is responsible for administering the nondiscrimination laws. Using past rulings like those in the above cases, they set guidelines for employers. The major guidelines that impinge on performance appraisal are:

- Companies may not use any selection device that discriminates against a protected group.
- The company does not have to intend to discriminate. It's enough if the selection device or procedure discriminates against a disproportionate number of people in a protected group.
- These rules apply to any practice that influences any employment decision, that is, selection, training, transfer, promotion, or termination.

In essence the guidelines require that any test or practice used to make employment decisions be valid or job related. Of course, like most of the requirements of these laws, this makes good business sense. I was once put in charge of validating employment tests for a company, back in the early 1970s when the idea of such validation was as new as the federal requirements were. The managers complained bitterly that the government was "interfering" with company practices. But, needless to say, we went ahead and did the statistical validation of the tests. And we found that one of them had a correlation coefficient of –.47, which means roughly that people who did well on the test did poorly on the job. What we found was that a test the company had been using to pick candidates selected people who were not good at the job. I think the feds did that company a favor by making them get rid of that invalid test. If the regulations hadn't come along, they would probably still be looking for high scorers on a useless test.

How Can a Manager Stay Legal?

I've given you all this information about the law because I think that knowing about it will help you stay on the right side of it. The practices recommended in this book will result in performance appraisals that are not only productive but also legal.

In most companies the personnel officer is responsible for seeing that the company's practices are legal. If you have any doubt about what you are about to do, check it with the experts in your company *beforehand.*

Here are some rules to follow:

- Document the reasons for all employment decisions—positive or negative.

- Always base your appraisals on specific, clearly communicated job requirements. It is best if these are written.
- Never appraise an employee if you are unfamiliar with the job requirements or have insufficient contact to make valid judgments.
- Avoid making subjective appraisals of an employee's personal characteristics.
- Never say anything in your appraisals about the employee's race, creed, color, sex, handicap, national origin, or veteran status.
- Base your appraisal on a number of observations; don't write a negative appraisal just after the employee has made an unusual mistake.
- Keep appraisal records private, between you and the employee and others who have a right to see them.
- Allow the employee to see the appraisal and to appeal it if he or she thinks it is unfair.
- Don't write negative references unless you can prove the information is correct or you may get sued for defamation.

What the law requires in performance appraisal will change over time. Keep abreast of changes. It's a cliché by now but true nonetheless: Open communication will foster understanding between you and your employees and help keep you out of court.

Chapter 11

Keeping on Top of It

I don't know what the future of performance appraisal will be. The only consensus I get from the experts I talk to is that it will grow in importance. There are a few trends that contribute to this belief.

More people have come to believe that it is their basic right to have a voice in decisions that affect their lives. This trend will continue, and future workers, even more than today's, will expect to be treated with fairness and with respect for their wishes, their ideas, and their privacy. We can expect these workers to challenge decisions made without their input. Performance appraisals will be a major target of these challenges if they are thought to be unfair. The challenges will come from a work force that is better educated, more aware, and more likely to probe for answers, to question authority, and to seek self-fulfillment.

If we are going to successfully manage this work force, we must develop sensitivities that weren't necessarily part of a manager's skills in the past. Years ago managers needed skills of planning, organizing, and leading. These skills will continue to be needed, but now and in the future we must develop an awareness of the interpersonal and political ramifications of our actions.

Some managers bemoan this change. They long for the docile, obedient workers of the past. But if you look at the changes in the right light, you will see they are for the better. Better educated, thoughtful, challenging employees can bring more to the job. If we can succeed in giving them the participation they want, we can elicit a commitment based on the satisfaction of important mutual needs. This can be a source of great energy and creative output. For managers who can learn to tap the energy and creativity, the satisfactions will be great. We as managers, of course, will be part of this trend ourselves, seeking the same levels of participation and the same respect of those who manage us.

In the future employees and managers will be more likely to work in separate places. Many futurists foresee a day when many information workers will be able to work in remote locations, linked to their corporate offices by communications and information processing equipment. The technology to make this possible is already here. This means that, as is the case with sales managers today, managers will have less daily contact with their people. We will have to be clever about inventing systems to keep ourselves informed and in contact. We will have to get better and better at the kind of specific work planning espoused in this book if we are to successfully evaluate people who will be working outside of today's normal office environment.

We can expect that due process will gain ever wider application in the workplace. The trends toward more involvement will probably have a legal side. Our performance appraisal decisions will more and more have to undergo the scrutiny of fairness committees and courts.

In the face of these and many other changes, all our management systems will have to either adjust or become dysfunctional. Systems that are working well today will need to be overhauled to keep up with society's changes.

Nonmanagers will not notice nor will they respond to the need for change. They will continue to use old methods long after they have become obsolete, and the changes they do make will be random and, as usual, too little too late. Those who take a casual attitude to their management jobs will not be ready for the future. The managers who watch for the signs of change will be ready to make the most of the opportunities; they will not become the victims of obsolescence.

Some Final Cautions
and Encouragements

None of the predictions I've made here are startling, nor is my advice surprising. The trends have already begun. Participation is already a strong value. Employees are already demanding a greater voice and more useful feedback. I have attempted to give you the means to provide both. Employees need as well as want these things. Without performance appraisal some will think our silence "gives consent" and will continue to behave in ways that are not necessarily productive. Others will think the absence of approval means that a change is necessary, and they may give up behaviors that are right on the mark. Without a positive response for their efforts, our best people will give up and go look elsewhere for a more appreciative boss.

Effective performance appraisal is hard. It requires skill, dedication, and time. But remember we are not talking about an aspect of management here. Planning, organizing, and controlling work are the core of your job.

To the extent that we shirk or are slipshod in managing our people, we risk harming them. We can make a wrong decision that will adversely affect another person's life and psychological well-being. Fairness and ethics require that we do our best.

Remember though that if this system of planning, follow-up, and appraisal is new to you, you have to give yourself a fair chance to learn it. Don't become discouraged if it doesn't work perfectly for you the first or second time. Take a while to get used to the new techniques, analyze what works best for you, and stick with your determination to get it right. In the long run you will.

Appendix

Overview of the Planning and Appraisal Process

Objectives	Procedure	Outcomes
Step One: Planning		
To decide on and communicate work expectations To plan performance improvement and personal growth goals	Employee and manager prepare their ideas and meet to decide mutually on the plan and set priorities	A written work plan that lays out specific tasks and objectives for the employee A list of support activities for the manager A follow-up schedule
Step Two: Follow-up*		
To evaluate interim progress To revise expectations if necessary	Employee and manager share perceptions of progress, discuss and solve problems, and change plans where needed	A revised work plan Renewed commitment
Step Three: Appraisal†		
To evaluate the work To analyze reasons for success or failure To plan for the next period	Employee and manager evaluate progress and meet to discuss their perceptions, assess the past period, and make a new plan	A plan for the next cycle Information to be used in making salary decisions, and so on, if this is needed

* This may occur several times during one planning and appraisal cycle.
† Salary action is done separately.

Index

ABOUT THE AUTHOR

A top-flight communications consultant since 1972 and president of her own firm, Patricia King has two decades' experience in designing and teaching training programs in management and communications skills. Among her clients are General Foods Corporation, Chase Manhattan Bank, E. R. Squibb & Sons, and J. Walter Thompson. With on-the-job experience in human resources planning and affirmative action at several large firms, Patricia King is a contributor to a major affirmative action text and also the author of *Mind to Disk to Paper, The New Secretary,* and *Never Work for a Jerk.*